# Say Something!

# Say Something!

## WRITING ESSAYS THAT MAKE THE GRADE

*Laura Swart*

*With illustrations by Barbara Lamb*

19 20 21 22 23 5 4 3 2 1

Printed and manufactured in Canada



**Brush Education Inc.**
www.brusheducation.ca
contact@brusheducation.ca

Cover design: Dean Pickup; Cover images: Robert Byron/Dreamstime.com
Interior design: Carol Dragich, Dragich Design
Copyediting: Leslie Vermeer


**Library and Archives Canada Cataloguing in Publication**
Swart, Laura, 1963-, author
Say something! : writing essays that make the grade / Laura Swart with illustrations by Barbara Lamb.

Issued in print and electronic formats.

ISBN 978-1-55059-779-0 (softcover).–ISBN 978-1-55059-780-6 (PDF).
–ISBN 978-1-55059-781-3 (Kindle).–ISBN 978-1-55059-782-0 (EPUB)

1. Essay-Authorship. 2. Report writing. 3. English language-Rhetoric. I. Title.

PE1471.S93 2018 808'.042 C2018-906572-9 C2018-906573-7

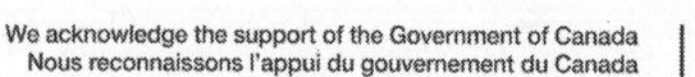

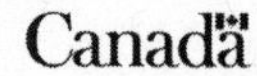

*In essay writing, the combinations of your words have to be,*
*in Timothy Findley's words,*
*"as precise as the combinations of gestures used by a dancer."*

# Acknowledgements

I am not the sole author of this book, though my name is on the cover. Lauri Seidlitz composed all of the "Editorial Eye" boxes and spent countless hours revising the manuscript. Leslie Vermeer's keen editing eye and passion for writing and teaching elevated the manuscript and encouraged me as a teacher and a writer. I am grateful to you both. Many thanks to the entire Brush team for your expertise and poignant feedback.

I am profoundly indebted to my daughter, Anika Swart, and to my students Timothy Harder, Ben Coxson, Grace Iverson, Isaac Ritskes, Nicole Achari, and Beth Dick for providing the writing samples that I needed to teach the principles in this book. It's been a delight to work with each one of you.

Abigail Red, thank you for taking the time to discuss the student essays with me. I always learn something when I'm in conversation with you. Robert Lacey, thank you for your generosity, for your intuitive writing. Barbara Lamb, for your beauty and your powerful gifts. You shine.

And praise be to El Roi, who gives us life, and love, and liberty.

# Contents

# Introduction

In *Say Something! Writing Essays That Make the Grade*, you'll discover what writing is and who you are as a writer. Words don't just appear on the page—writing is hard work. As Hans-Georg Gadamer puts it, it comes from being around; in the process of writing, something emerges that extends beyond your control.

We learn to write largely by imitating others—not by producing copies, but by understanding *essence*. Reading evocative texts, then, both creative and analytical pieces, is critical if you want to gain the skills and confidence necessary to express yourself in unencumbered, detailed prose.

But there are barriers along the way—impediments, setbacks, limitations.

To overcome them, you must acquaint yourself with the rhetorical, structural, and stylistic properties of academic essay writing. Initially this exploration will involve debunking a few myths about the writing event: that a piece of writing is a box you put stuff in; that you must begin at the beginning and end at the end; that outlines always precede drafts; that low grades are a symptom of mediocrity; that the writer somehow dominates the writing event.

There are many types of essays, but in this book, we'll focus on those that employ analytical rather than scientific modes of investigation—essays that are assigned in humanities and social sciences courses such as history, philosophy, religion, and literature. We'll move through the essay-writing process four times—in four *takes*, as it were, with each take gaining in detail and complexity—and we'll discover how to produce powerful pieces of writing, examining common errors that post-secondary students make when they compose.

By the end of the book, you will be able to do the following:

- define who you are as a writer and use your gifts to create powerful pieces of writing;
- read critically, ask effective questions, and grapple with difficult texts;
- determine the rhetorical situation for each writing event and contextualize pieces appropriately;
- develop an effective writing process—from exploring, to creating, to revising and editing;

- write analytical papers with persuasive thesis statements and supporting theoretical arguments;
- use appropriate source materials, ensuring that quotations are relevant, poignant, and seamless;
- extend the boundaries of your thinking, giving a wide berth to mundane, ubiquitous ideas; and
- improve your grades, whether your writing woes are minimal or substantial.

The bottom line is this: writing takes confidence. You have to believe that you have something to say. Søren Kierkegaard, the father of existentialism, puts it this way: "Be that self which one truly is."

# *TAKE ONE*

In our first take on essay writing, we'll focus on who you are as a writer, veering away from the stiff conventions that you perhaps were taught in high school. I'll introduce you to the essentials of essay writing—pointing out some of the more egregious errors I see in post-secondary writing—and teach you how to avoid them.

# 1

# The Who

Who are you? The infamous question posed by the classic rock band The Who is pertinent to essay writing, it turns out. Some writers like to free fall: they begin at the beginning, end at the end, and make no stops in between. Others need structured, detailed outlines to guide them. I do a lot of drafting in my head while I'm picking saskatoons by the river.

I'm also a verbal processor, so I focus more on the beat of my sentences than on diction or even meaning. What about you? Are you a visual or a tactile learner? Are you studying law? Engineering?

*There is no right way to write.*

Fine arts? Do you prefer facts and figures or abstract ideas? Do you dislike or thrive on ambiguity? Your answers to these questions are manifested in literate gestures, as Timothy Findlay puts it, and affect how you think, how you learn, how you compose.

Writers such as Ernest Hemingway and John Steinbeck construct clean sentences with profound ideas; others, like Hans-Georg Gadamer or Michel Foucault, create mazes, not sentences—and writers like Friedrich Nietzsche bring entire worlds into every paragraph.

There is no right way to write, despite what you perhaps have heard to the contrary. *You* are the writer: *to thine own self be true*, Polonius says. You cannot contort the writing event—it won't bear the tension. You need to discover what's inside of you and learn how to extract it.

In essence, you need to develop your *writing voice*.

Many artists begin the process by imitating others. Eric Clapton, for example, imitated Big Bill Broonzy and Muddy Waters until he found a sound of his own. In Michelangelo's time, painters worked as apprentices, imitating the works of their masters. Most writers immerse themselves in texts that model what they want to learn. I go to John Steinbeck for imagery, Joseph Conrad for syntax, and John Updike for dialogue. I also read Indigenous poetry because it is compressed and lyrical, and I want my own writing to have a similar sound. Reading, I would say, has the single greatest impact on developing writing skills; it is just as important as writing itself.

And yes, I'm talking about reading both fiction and nonfiction to improve your essays. Your course textbooks are inadequate models—unless, of course, you want to sound like an encyclopedia. But how often do you think your professors read Wikipedia for pleasure? Find good authors—authors whom you enjoy—and spend fifteen minutes a day with them. When you finish a book, read it again. The syntax and images and ideology will infuse your mind, and your writing will begin its metamorphosis.

The issue is not about *the* way to write or *the* way to construct an essay or even about what the quintessential essay looks like. Certainly, there are expectations in academia and strategies for writing well. We'll get to those. But you must learn how to maximize your strengths and shape your weaknesses so they serve your ideas rather than hinder them. And to do that, you must follow the wisdom of Polonius.

## 2

# Writing as Trinity

But here's the rub: you're not the only player in the game.

The writing event is a trinity of sorts: writer, reader, and text. Let's first discuss that ubiquitous character, the reader. In university, students are zeroed-in on readership. They want to get the grade, so they write what they think the professor wants to hear—and that requires a sprinkle of clairvoyance. But nothing will stifle your writing more than writing solely for the reader. Your piece will feel more like a simulation than a live event if you obsess about the person on the other end, because the writing won't come from *you*.

Look at it this way. When you conduct research for an academic essay, the texts that you study are *alive*; they're not events of the past. Every time a reader enters into a text, she adds a layer of meaning to it; thus, although the author and professor wield a level of authority and understanding, they are not the sole proprietors of the text's meaning. Each reader has an analysis as valuable as the professor's—*if* her analysis is rooted in the text, and *if* she has studied the text, moved around in it, and understands it. Some of my students have proffered analyses of my own writing that are more intriguing than my original intent.

Don't underestimate *your* relationship with course texts. Your ideas, your voice, your diction and syntax *matter* and are integral to your analysis. At the same time, don't forget who you are writing for: an intelligent human being who carries a mantle of expertise, who wants to be engaged—and who likely is grading a foot-high stack of essays under a table lamp at one o'clock in the morning. Don't sedate him with gutless sentences and ideas. Here are a few examples of gutless sentences I've encountered in the last few years:

- An American president wields great influence.
- The *Canadian Oxford Dictionary* defines community as ....
- Capitalism and communism are poles apart in their implications for governance.
- Europe has undergone substantial changes throughout history.

Some professors want you to assume nothing, define everything. But in most cases, be assured that after decades of research, teaching, and publishing, your professor likely has at least a rudimentary understanding of his subject area and wants you to do one thing: say something. Take a risk. Make your essay stand out from the other 54 that he must grade before slipping beneath his downy comforter.

3

# The Writing Process

Hemingway rewrote the ending to *A Farewell to Arms* 47 times.

Yet if you go online and read a few essays, you'll get the impression that the writer scratched out a draft, corrected a few spelling errors, and submitted the essay. What you don't see is the sweat and tears that created that essay—if it's a good one.

Writing is difficult. It's like a bull terrier that yanks on the leash—not a German shepherd that obeys your every command. As Jacques Derrida says, "When I write, there is a feeling of necessity, of something that is stronger than myself that demands that I must write as I do." That thing pulling at you, demanding

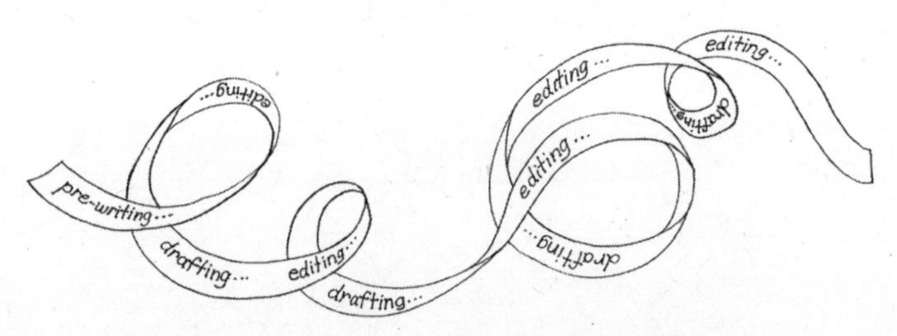


*Writing is a circular process. You move back and forth and up and down until you see something intelligible emerging.*

something of you, takes time to create. It's a circular process involving prewriting, drafting, and editing; you move back and forth and up and down until you see something intelligible emerging.

Most writers do *some* form of prewriting before drafting; it saves time and helps them to generate and organize ideas. You've heard about prewriting before: listing, mapping, outlining, the five Ws. It's about *quantity*, not quality—not structure, not paragraphs, not content.

If you've found a method of prewriting that works for you, stay with it. But I'd like you to try something called *freewriting*, which works well for people with writer's block or weak grammar or who lack confidence in their writing ability. Many of these writers are afraid of producing substandard writing, but in freewriting, they at least get something on the page.

Find a pen and paper or a computer. Take a deep breath and complete the following.

1. In **two** minutes, respond to the following essay question: *Describe the strengths of a democratic system of government.*
2. After two minutes of writing, put down your pen and count your words.

How many did you get? Nineteen words? Eight? In a typical classroom, my students will approach this task in different ways. Some write about a current event related to democracy. Others write about issues, such as people who vote without being informed or politicians who break campaign promises; still others speak abstractly (*there are no perfect people, even though people create democracy*). Some might list their questions about democracy. But all of my students find it difficult to generate more than a dozen or so words.

Yet in two minutes, the average person can type 80 to 200 words.

Freewriting is writing without stopping, writing without punctuating—dare I say writing without thinking? Take a few seconds to think about the topic, and then begin. *Do not* stop under any circumstances. If you get stuck, repeat the last word you wrote wrote wrote wrote until something comes to mind. Let's try it.

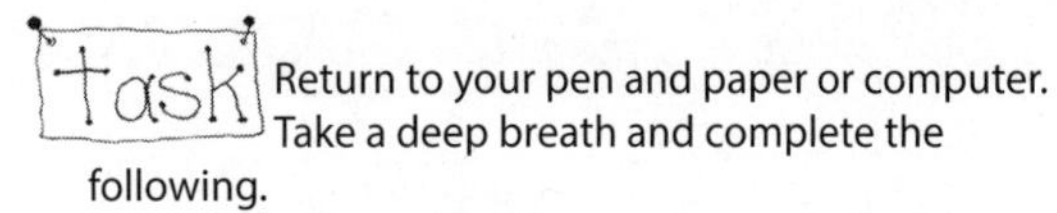


Return to your pen and paper or computer. Take a deep breath and complete the following.

1. In **two** minutes, respond to the following essay question: *Describe the strengths of a communist system of government.*
2. After two minutes of freewriting, put down your pen and count your words.

How many did you get this time? Most of my students at least triple their word count.

And the amazing thing is this: you have a draft! Now you have to do stuff with it. We'll get to that.

But before we move on, I'd like to mention that *talking* is an effective form of prewriting, especially for auditory learners and verbal processors. After writing a draft, find someone who will listen to you read it, preferably someone you know—or perhaps someone you *don't* know, such as someone sitting beside you on the subway—and have the person ask you questions after the reading. You'll be astounded by how many errors you find, how many holes, and your listener's questions will help you to flesh out ideas and find strengths in your writing.

It is particularly important to understand the writing process—and who you are as a writer—in a timed, in-class exam. If you've been given one hour to write an essay, you need to know in advance how much time you require for prewriting, drafting, and editing. I have difficulty generating ideas, but once the light goes on, I can flesh out a draft quite quickly. Therefore, I would take at least one-third of the allotted time for prewriting. Other people are brimming with ideas but don't know how to articulate them; they need more time for drafting. If you struggle with English grammar, you need at least fifteen minutes to edit.

Let's now talk about entry-level essays.

# 4

# Entry-Level Essays

## *The Five-Paragraph Style*

Some people call this the five-paragraph essay: it's a predictable, formulaic piece of writing, and it's *everywhere*. It goes something like this.

Every essay has three main parts: an introduction, a body (which contains three-to-five paragraphs), and a conclusion.

The introduction begins with a hook, a sentence that *hooks* the reader, as it were (macabre as that metaphor might be), with a statistic, quotation, or short anecdote. After the hook come one or two descriptive sentences of dubious purpose that lead into the thesis statement—the Lord of the essay, the *raison d'etre*—which occupies the final sentence of the introduction. The thesis likely contains a controlling idea—an inventory of what is coming—because your professor, being rather aged, has little to no short-term memory and needs to have this controlling idea stated several times throughout the essay.

Enter the body. Each paragraph begins with a topic sentence that emphatically states the main idea of the paragraph: no ambiguity, no loose ends. Following are five to seven sentences that employ statistics, facts, and quotations to support the topic sentence. Then there is a kind of concluding sentence to reiterate the main idea.

Finally comes the concluding paragraph, an inversion of the introduction. It first restates the thesis, because as I stated earlier, the professor has by this time forgotten what it is. It ends with an erudite final sentence that wraps everything up and titillates the reader for several seconds after the reading. The conclusion is about half the length of the introduction, because no one is certain about what it should say.

Students who graduate from this structure and move on to post-secondary education simply toss in a few additional body paragraphs, depending on the required length of the essay.

Essays like this are *easy*! You can knock one off in a few hours: say what you're going to say, say it, say what you said. As far as the writing process goes, always write the thesis and introduction first. Then write the body, then the conclusion. Oh—and write an outline before you begin. (But didn't Michel Foucault ask, "If you knew when you began a book what you would say at the end, do you think that you would have the courage to write it?")

And as far as readership is concerned? Pretend you're writing for a twelve-year-old.

The five-paragraph style is a good starter essay: it teaches you how to structure your thoughts around a controlling idea. We can perhaps justify this method in oral storytelling or grade school, but in post-secondary education, you have to *think*.

So then. I want to give you a few preliminaries about essay *structure*—the substructure, if you will—before we move into the complexities of essay writing.

5

# Anatomy of an Essay

## *Viva Puffs and Oreos*

I'll begin by talking briefly about cookies. Not web cookies, but cookies that you can actually eat: Viva Puffs and Oreos. Which

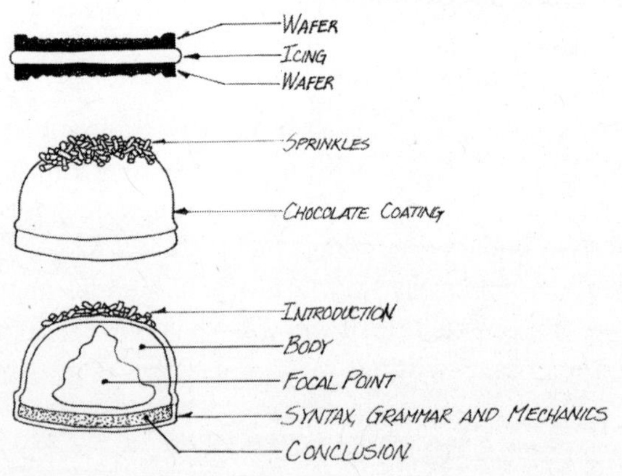


*Viva Puffs are a more apt metaphor for essay structure than Oreos are.*

type of cookie do you think best represents correct essay structure? If you guessed Oreos, you guessed wrong—and you've possibly been conditioned by five-paragraph teaching: you favour rigid lines and equal portions.

Viva Puffs, it turns out, are a more apt metaphor for essay structure. The sprinkles on the top are the introduction: they entice you, draw you in. The marshmallow is the body. It is significantly larger than the introduction and conclusion, and it can't be separated into parts: it's seamless. The jam—the thesis—is the focal point of the cookie, threading its way from top to bottom, widening as it goes. The wafer at the base is the conclusion. It's made partially of sugar, like the sprinkles, but notice that it does not replicate the sprinkles. And finally, the chocolate coating is the syntax, grammar, and mechanics—it holds everything together (if you can't write a sentence, your essay will be unpalatable). Keep this Viva Puff in mind; we'll be returning to it throughout the book.

# 6

# An Imaginary Essay

Suppose you've been asked to write about the evils of smoking. After several hours of thought, you compose an alluring thesis: *Smoking is bad for your health*. Your three main paragraphs will develop the following arguments: smoking is bad for your social life; smoking is bad for your physical health; smoking is bad for your mental health.

You quickly drum up an outline—thankfully, little thought is required because the argument against smoking has existed for so many years that it is palpable.

Does your outline look anything like this?

**Introduction**

- Opening remarks
- Thesis: Smoking is bad for your health.

**Body paragraph 1**: First, smoking is bad for your social life.

- Isolation
- Lack of interest in activities
- Public perception

**Body paragraph 2**: Second, smoking is bad for your physical health.

- Cardiovascular disease
- Respiratory disease
- Cancer

**Body paragraph 3**: Finally, smoking is bad for your mental health.

- Stress
- Anxiety
- Depression

**Conclusion**

- Thesis: Smoking is bad for your health.
- Closing remarks

Converting this outline into an essay is easy; you open with a hook: a statistic divulging the annual number of deaths related to cigarette smoking. Each paragraph begins with a transition, a word such as *first*, *second*, *third*—or even something more provocative like *In addition* or *Another reason*—and then delivers a litany of statistics to support the thesis. You conclude the essay by reiterating the thesis and urging readers to change their behaviour: *Smoking is bad, so don't do it.*

It's all so neat and tidy! But does this look like an essay that you would want to dive into? Perhaps not. I'm being facetious, of course, but let's humour each other a little longer and examine the structure of this essay.

## Cut and Paste Rule

Let's speak in terms of arguments rather than paragraphs, because an argument can comprise several paragraphs. How should you order the arguments? You could begin, as I have, by describing the social stigma of smoking; then you could move into the physical health argument with a catchy transition such as *Another reason that smoking is bad is that it impacts physical health*. The third argument could begin with *A final reason that smoking is bad is that it affects mental health*.

Does the order of arguments really matter? Many contend that the strongest argument should appear first in the body to entice the reader; others place it at the end to leave a lasting impression. Some writers try to couch weak arguments somewhere in the middle. But really, there shouldn't *be* any weak arguments in an academic essay: everything you say should be prodigious.

In a great essay, you can't move things around; you can't cut and paste an argument, a paragraph, or even a sentence without damaging the whole. Remember our Viva Puff marshmallow? You can't take it apart like an Oreo: it's seamless. But in my smoking essay, it makes little difference whether I begin with the physical, emotional, or social impacts of smoking.

## Natural and Artificial Transitions

The arguments in my smoking essay are *forced* together with artificial transitions such as *first, in addition,* and *finally*. Such

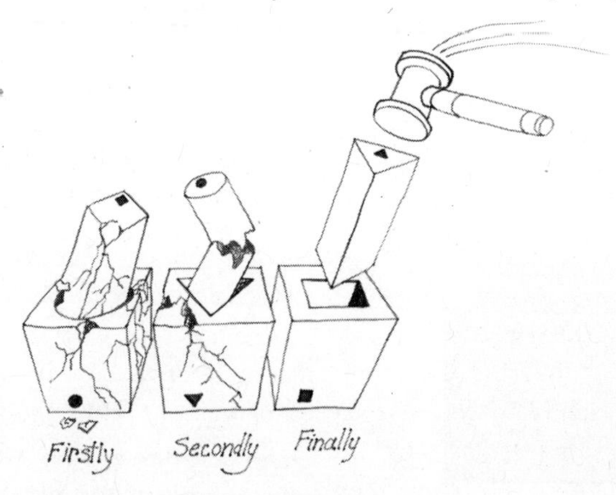


*Don't force an argument together with artificial transitions.*

transitions are necessary only if your professor failed grade six mathematics or if you are writing a rather long piece and want to remind your reader of where you've been or where you're going. In a shorter essay of 1000 to 2000 words, they need not make more than one or two appearances. You *do* need transitions, but you need *natural* transitions—and that's how you build a body that looks like a marshmallow.

*Piece your argument together so the parts flow naturally into one another.*

So then. Think about creating flow and piecing together arguments that build on one another thematically or contextually. If we return to our smoking essay, we can make a few changes. There seems to be a logical connection between mental health and the ability to socialize, so I'll paste those two arguments together. But where does physical health come in? I cannot simply slap it on the hind quarters of the essay like pinning the tail on a donkey. It has to *fit*. It turns out, however, that physical and mental well-being are yoked together, so the order of my arguments could look like this:

**Argument 1**: Smoking impairs your physical health.

- Cardiovascular disease
- Respiratory disease
- Cancer

**Argument 2**: These physical problems can affect mental health.

- Stress
- Anxiety
- Depression

**Argument 3**: If mental health is impaired, your social life may be affected.

- Lack of interest in activities
- Isolation
- Public perception

In the third argument, I changed the order to *Lack of interest in activities* and *Isolation*. It seems more logical that mental illness curtails people's interest in activities, leading to isolation.

Here, then, is the thrust of the essay: smoking causes physical health problems that can lead to stress, anxiety, and depression—and mental health issues often isolate people by decreasing their desire for social engagement. These ideas are inexorably linked—all except my final point about public perception. You will sometimes find yourself in this situation, where one or more arguments is incompatible with the others.

You have three options: make it fit (perhaps being isolated changes people's perception of you), eliminate it and build on your other arguments, or if it works, pull ideas out of the body and put them in the conclusion or introduction. This is one reason that I prefer to write my introductions last.

This example is, of course, an oversimplification. And there are different ways of arranging the arguments. For example, current research indicates that mental illnesses literally imprint themselves on the physical body, impairing pathways in the brain and changing the way the body functions. To make this argument, I would place mental health before physical health. Perhaps I would say that smoking isolates people and isolation triggers mental health problems, which imprint themselves on the physical body—and I could say in the conclusion that these imprints are passed on to successive generations.

I now have a beautifully cohesive structure, but the content is as flat as Oreo icing—it's not a lovely, rounded marshmallow. This is because the thesis is not debatable (perhaps in the 1920s the topic would have been hotly debated) and the essay is illogical; it's unlikely that smoking cigarettes causes multi-generational mental health problems.

My point is this: when arguments and sentences flow naturally from one to the next, artificial transitions aren't necessary, and the essay can't be taken apart—it therefore complies with our Cut and Paste rule.

## Bleeding Paragraphs

Inherent to the Cut and Paste rule is this: ideas in one paragraph shouldn't bleed into another. For example, in my argument about physical health, I shouldn't lament the isolated hospital room that smoking will land me in unless I intend to use isolation as a transition between arguments about the physical and social impacts of smoking.

In short, each argument should be distinct.

This perhaps is self-evident, but sometimes when you are writing a longer, more complex essay, organization and flow can be difficult to create. In such cases, I use letters to label my ideas in the prewriting stage. For example, I might put a *p* beside each fact pertaining to physical health and an *s* beside facts pertaining to social life, and then cut and paste like letters together.

## Lopsided Essays

One problem I often find in student essays is that introductions and conclusions are disproportionately long, leaving little room for the lofty arguments of the body. Here's a rule of thumb: for a four-page essay, the introduction and conclusion should be about half a page each. For essays that are eight to ten pages in length, the introduction and conclusion can be longer—about a page each. If you do the math, you'll deduce that the introduction and conclusion should each make up approximately 12.5 percent of the essay.

---

In Take One, I've outlined some of the more glaring deficiencies I see in student essays. In short, I've described C- and D-level essays: those that are forced, predictable, and hollowed out. I've also talked about natural transitions and the Cut and Paste rule, which start you on the path toward essay improvement. If you are wondering how to move your grades up and over the bell curve, take a breath—and turn the page.

# *TAKE TWO*

Because learning occurs through repetition, this book will loop through the essay-writing process three more times: once with the Bedouin in Saudi Arabia, once with Moroccans in Marrakech, and once with a menagerie of people and places. Each loop will bring us deeper into the process, and in the end, after repeated exposure to principles of essay writing with increasing levels of complexity, you'll learn how to write a truly remarkable essay.

7

# Writing a Critical Essay

Critical thinking is at the core of all learning and academia, and a critical essay is a critique of one or more literary texts. Michel Foucault defines the critique this way: "A critique does not consist in saying that things aren't good the way they are. It consists in seeing on just what type of assumptions, of familiar notions, of

*The goal of a critical essay is to convince readers that your claims are true or valid based on the evidence you provide.*

established and unexamined ways of thinking the accepted practices are based."

Most essay assignments in the humanities involve critiquing texts and constructing arguments—in essence, making claims about meaning and supporting them with textual evidence. A claim might be an opinion, a proposal, an evaluation, a cause-and-effect statement, or an interpretation. The goal of a critical essay is to convince readers that your claims are true or valid based on the evidence that you provide.

Let's read a simple yet profound text, "Bedouin" from Robert Lacey's *The Kingdom*, and write a critical essay in response. You'll find "Bedouin" in Appendix 1, page 186; please read it carefully before proceeding.

I'll give you a somewhat benign essay question: *Describe the social structure of Bedouin culture in 1891.* If you were to write an entry-level essay in response to this question, you would first produce a thesis, and there is a high probability that you'd come up with something like this: *Bedouin social structure revolves around three main groups: men, women, and children.* If you were feeling particularly spunky, you might enlarge the statement like this: *Bedouin social structure is one of division, with different roles assigned to men, women, and children.* You would then knock off a few body paragraphs describing the roles of the various players—being careful to support your claims with evidence from the text—and conclude the essay by restating the thesis and crafting one or two clever sentences that leave your readers dreaming about camels and dung beetles.

In this scenario, *you* are the master of the essay. You are in control. You have become, if I may refer to Foucault, an essay fascist: "The strategic adversary is fascism ... the fascism in us all, in our heads and in our everyday behavior, the fascism that causes us to love power, to desire the very thing that dominates and exploits us." Indeed, such an essay *does* exploit in the end: it lands you precisely in the middle of the bell curve—a comfortable place, certainly, but a place where you are akin to an assembly-line worker pumping out worn-out metaphors that are, in Nietzsche's words, without sensuous power.

*Some essays will land you in the middle of the bell curve; their language and ideas are comfortable and predictable—but lacking power.*

To write well, you must place greater demands on yourself and on your piece, subjecting your ideas to interrogation and *ref-ormation*—or *reformationem,* which in the Latin form means "to shape again." In the following five steps, I'll describe a different essay-writing process, and as you read, I'd like you to examine your assumptions, familiar notions, and unexamined ways of think-ing, as Foucault would say, in order to break them up and find other ways of thinking. Although I'm narrowing in on critical essays to teach these steps, they apply to all theoretical essays.

## Step 1: Understand the Question

Why do professors ask questions? Because, according to Gadamer, "the essence of the question is the opening up, and the keeping open, of possibilities." Thus, it is imperative that your essay be directed at the question posed. Self-evident, you say? Perhaps, but I've graded my share of essays that are way outside the fence line.

But allow me to digress. What if you are given a choice of questions?

Choose something compelling. Often, professors will toss in one or two elementary questions for students who struggle with essay writing. But mark this: a weak question begets a weak essay.

Don't write about worn-out topics unless they are in the news. Choose something you are passionate about, but not something that is *too* familiar; as Colum McCann says, "Don't write what you know; write toward what you want to know":

> Step out of your skin. Risk yourself. This opens up the world. Go to another place. Investigate what lies beyond your curtains, beyond the wall, beyond the corner, beyond your town, beyond the edges of your own known country.
>
> A writer is an explorer. She knows she wants to get somewhere, but she doesn't know if somewhere even exists yet. It is still to be created. A Galapagos of the imagination. A whole new theory of who we are.

*A writer is an explorer.*

Of course, once you conduct research, you will in a sense *know* the topic before you write a draft. But somehow, that wrestling, that struggle with words and ideas, will seep into your writing and make it real.

Try also to find topics that others are less likely to write about. Remember, in a class of 100 students choosing from four questions, the majority will gravitate toward the easiest question; thus, your professor will have read fifty essays about Hamlet's feigned insanity before he gets to yours. Are you certain your ideas are so profound, so unique, that his head won't be bobbing as he reads your essay?

So then. Choose a good topic—then make sure you understand the essay question.

Suppose you decide to write about the famed Foucault–Chomsky debate of 1971, applying theories about language acquisition to the dialogue in the novel *Ransomed*, by Laura Swart. (Be aware that some professors encourage students to use outside sources in critical essays; others do not).

Following are renditions of actual essay questions posed by university professors. Some questions are disjointed, as in the following example:

> Consider Foucault and Chomsky's theoretical observations about human nature (specifically in their discussion about social constructivism and the natural sciences) to explore Chomsky's example of universal grammar and specifically the laws of consonant mutation. Apply your findings to the dialogue in a novel of your choice.

Your first task is to highlight key words.

> Consider *Foucault* and *Chomsky's* theoretical observations about human nature (specifically, in their discussion about *social constructivism* and the *natural sciences*) to explore Chomsky's example of *universal grammar* and specifically, the laws of *consonant mutation*. *Apply* your findings to the *dialogue in a novel* of your choice.

Next, you need to locate the kernel—the operating system—of the question. What exactly is your professor asking? Ultimately, this question is about consonant mutation. This is what you are to explore—and in that exploration, you must use the dialogue in *Ransomed* as evidence to support your claims.

Here, in short, is what you will discuss in this essay.

> Foucault: how his theories about social constructivism and the natural sciences *apply to* universal grammar in general and consonant mutation in particular
>
> Chomsky: how his theories about social constructivism and the natural sciences *apply to* universal grammar in general and consonant mutation in particular

This question lends itself to a compare/contrast essay; thus, you will likely use the block method or the point-by-point method to unpack your weighty ideas.

### *Block method*

Using this method, your first argument will discuss *only* Foucault's theories; your second argument will discuss *only* Chomsky's theories (or the other way around).

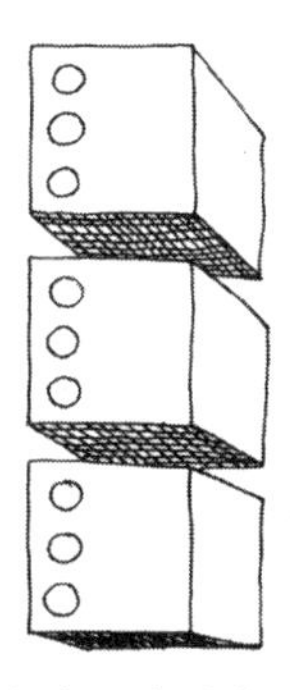

*The block method discusses all the points supporting each argument at one time.*

Foucault
- How his theories about social constructivism apply to universal grammar and specifically consonant mutation
- How his theories about the natural sciences apply to universal grammar and specifically consonant mutation

Chomsky

- How his theories about social constructivism apply to universal grammar and specifically consonant mutation
- How his theories about the natural sciences apply to universal grammar and specifically consonant mutation

The block method is the most common form of compare/contrast essay and is easier to write—and in most cases, easier for your reader to follow.

*Point-by-point method*

Alternately, you can use the point-by-point method to compare *theories*, not theorists. A point-by-point essay would look like this.

How social constructivism applies to universal grammar and consonant mutation

- Foucault
- Chomsky

How natural sciences apply to universal grammar and consonant mutation

- Foucault
- Chomsky

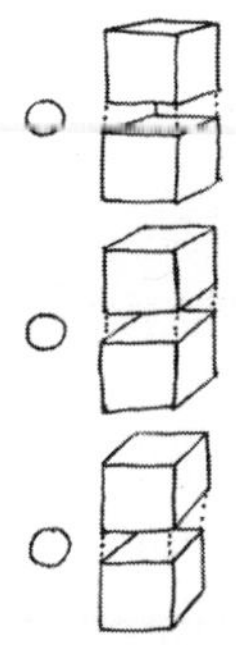

*The point-by-point method alternates the points supporting each argument.*

Once again, you would use the dialogue in *Ransomed* as evidence to support your claims. Notice that the structure is perfectly balanced; the order of ideas doesn't change from one argument to the next.

Here is another essay question pertaining to the same debate. I've highlighted key words and found the operating system.

> *Using a literary text that has been brought to the screen,* consider the remarks that *Foucault and Chomsky* make about human nature. What aspects of their views are *similar* and what aspects are *different? What do the differences reveal about* their respective theoretical approaches (i.e., *whether there is an innate human nature*)? Identify some of what you find to be the *strengths and weaknesses* of the respective approaches to analyzing your text (e.g., *what do these approaches allow us to see or what limits do they place on our understanding?*).

For this question (a wordy one indeed), you will discuss whether human nature is innate or a cultural construction. You will delineate Foucault's and Chomsky's theories using Alice, as she is portrayed Tim Burton's 2010 rendition of Wonderland, to discuss how Foucault would demonstrate that Alice is a cultural construct and how Chomsky would show that she has innate human nature. In essence, you will compare and contrast Foucault's and Chomsky's theories about human nature as they apply to Alice; in particular, you will discuss the strengths and weaknesses of each view, focussing on the extent to which they give us understanding about human nature. It is extremely important to answer every part of the question; thus, it might be helpful to break it into pieces.

Foucault: Alice is a cultural construct.

- Strengths and weaknesses of Foucault's position
- How his position affects our understanding

Chomsky: Alice possesses an innate human nature.

- Strengths and weaknesses of Chomsky's position
- How his position affects our understanding

Foucault and Chomsky compared and contrasted.

How do you order this menagerie of ideas? We'll discuss that at length in Take Four.

Please read the following essay question.

> Discuss Foucault and Chomsky's claims about the notion of objective truth. Use two literary texts to demonstrate which assumptions these respective claims share and which ones are points on which they depart from each other. Perhaps you could consider these texts with respect to *epistemological* (what and how we can know something) and *ontological* (the essence or nature of the world or beings) assumptions. Explain which of these assumptions are shared and which are not. Evaluate the relative strengths and weaknesses of these theoretical perspectives.

Not all questions are effectively worded; this one is dense and repetitive. However, with a little effort, you can decipher what the professor is asking you to do.

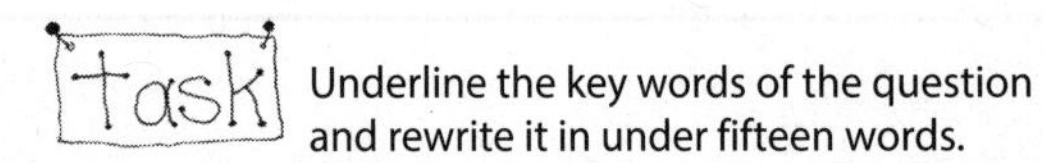


**Underline the key words of the question and rewrite it in under fifteen words.**

Some questions are too broad for the required length of the paper. For example, if you are asked to write a 750-word essay about France's class system in Stendhal's *The Red and the Black*, you should first narrow the topic, or your essay will be a mile wide and an inch deep. You could perhaps compare the dissatisfaction of an upper- and a lower-class character—but first get your professor's approval, and mention in the introduction that you'll be using case studies to examine the two classes.

## Step 2: Use the CSI Method

Let's now return to the comfort of our Bedouin tent. You have your question: *Describe the social structure of Bedouin culture in 1891*. Quite an amicable question, I would say, after having discoursed with Foucault and Chomsky about the essential questions of human existence.

Many students believe that writing an essay is like falling down a rabbit hole: bewildering at best. What goes on in the paragraphs? Argumentation, of course. But how do you write an argument? How do you integrate other people's ideas—your research—with your own writing? Where do you *begin*?

I'd like to propose that the essence of an essay is a series of **CSI**s: claims (**C**), support for those claims (**S**), and an investigation of the relationship between the support and claims (**I**). Your arguments might be comprised of **CSI**s, or **CSSI**s, or **CSCSI**s, but essentially, each argument is a series of **CSI**s: claim, support, and investigation.

*The essence of an essay is a series of CSIs: claims (C), support (S), and investigation (I).*

The **I**'s are difficult to produce because they require *thought*; they cannot be rattled off like a Trumponian tweet. It's relatively effortless to make the claim that Alice enters into a fantasy world, then list several examples to support that claim—talking animals and shrinking humans. But what if the world beneath the rabbit hole is, in fact, reality, and Alice's former existence was the imagined one? This is where the **I** comes in. Typically, **I**'s are necessary when claims are strong; weak claims don't require investigation or discussion: they just *are*. If your paper contains only **CS**s, your grades will not likely exceed anything above a B, or more likely, a C.

How then does one create a **CSI** paper?

### *Support: Collect data*

Your first task is *not* to construct a thesis.

Rather, begin by collecting all the data, all the support (the **S** in **CSI**) in the text that is related to the question. By *support* I mean that which is written directly in the text. The method you use depends on your preferred mode of prewriting (see Take One); I prefer to create lists or charts.

Try to be impartial in this process: don't impose your biases on the text by squeezing data into prefabricated boxes. Simply allow the data to speak. Later, you will organize it, make claims about it, and ultimately write a thesis statement and an essay.

> task Given our essay question, *Describe the social structure of Bedouin culture in 1891*, please extract from the text all the data related to social structure. Make a list of all the interactions between men, women, and children.

In this task, perhaps you began, as many of my students have, with comments like this:

**Men**

Waited on

Engage in the coffee routine

Follow rituals

Sit on a carpet

Held in higher esteem than women and boy

**Women**

Serve the men

Unseen

Distribute provisions

Subservient

**Boy**

Serves the men

Works hard

Skilled and efficient

These remarks are cursory at best. If you want to write a strong essay, you must take time to examine the text sentence by sentence and word by word, constantly asking questions about why the author chooses some words over others, what the words mean contextually, and what their larger meanings are. For example, why do the men "saunter" rather than "walk"? What does "sauntering" suggest about life in exile? You must discover how to *look*, as Timothy Findley puts it, to unearth latent things that others don't see. In the work of a good writer, no detail is by chance; everything feeds into the overall impression and meaning.

Notice that there are two claims in the list: that women are subservient and that men are held in higher esteem than the women and boy. These things are not written in the text and require support and investigation (**SI**) to be validated. We could also argue that the text never *states* that the boy works hard or is skilled, but these details are irrefutable and would not make strong claims.

Without being too pedantic, try not to confuse claims and support at this stage.

Please read the following transcript of a few students extracting data from the text. Notice that they are constantly asking questions and thinking about claims as they read.

**Boy**

Boy is in front of the tent, on a carpet.

Carpet. Is the carpet a luxury? Carpet is rich, luxury, richly woven.

How significant is the goat hair?

Boy is preparing coffee. Does coffee mean anything in Saudi cultures? Often very significant, bonding. Need to research these things. He makes the coffee, and coffee seems important to the social structure of society.

Boy is surrounded by animals: cantankerous camels, goats.

There are grey and black colours so far.

Boy is associated with cold wind, grey sky.

No girls.

Boy calls for water. Does this give him authority? No words in response; only action. Only boy speaks: speech associated with boy. What does speech signify? He doesn't speak to the men, only the women.

Puts wood on fire; he is associated with fire. What is fire? Heat, light, life. He's feeding the fire.

Boy is associated with hot and cold.

Boy is a servant.

Preparing for manhood: is this true or an assumption?

Blackened brass, boiling. What is brass? Beauty and luxury? Maybe in our culture, but what about Saudi Arabia in the 1800s?

Beans are green (like the boy?), also brown, pale, dry, emit aroma after roasting (fire).

Verbs associated with the boy: *toss*, *pound*, *strike*. This boy is the future; all these things are associated with the future.

Brass mortar, bell-like sound. Strong, strong images. You can hear the bell. In our culture, a bell is associated with church, music. Can we impose this meaning on Saudi culture? Rings, echoes. It's like a call, Pavlov's dog: creates a response. It goes everywhere and evokes change, shifts, movement—and the boy is doing it.

Pounds cardamom seeds into dust. What's the history of cardamom? Cardamom is very valuable, flavourful, pungent. All associated with the boy.

Water boils three times. Is three significant?

Date palm coil? Straining. Dates are sweet. Other significance? Find out.

Boy balances, right and left hand, important in Saudi culture. One hand is clean, the other is unclean. Cups in right hand, that's what men touch to their lips.

Walks in a circle. Inside or outside the circle?

Ritual, feels like.

Stands, waits for men to finish. Puts empties on bottom of stack.

He is Abdul Aziz ibn Sa'ud, the only person named. How is naming significant?

Founder of the Kingdom.

**Women**

Women are shut off: strong language.

Embroidery. What is embroidery? Compared with cross stitch? Is it delicate? Refined? Is it art in Saudi culture? It's a hanging.

Women have their own section.

Unidentifiable hands. No identity, interchangeable. Only hands mentioned: significance of hands?

They have the supplies, the unrefined goods.

Probably looking after children, but it's not in the text.

**Men**

Men are robed. Luxury? Nobility? Only clothing mentioned. If something is mentioned only once, it's important.

Respond to the bell.

Men saunter. Why don't they walk? Where are they sauntering to? The fire, the light.

Men lean on sheepskin. Luxury? Leisure? How is sheepskin different from goat skin? White versus black?

Bare feet. Cross legged.

Men are associated with sun, warm, colour, slowness.

Hold out their cups when they want more coffee; waggle cups from side to side when they've had enough.

Men don't speak in the text; they don't address the boy or the women.

There are also several details about the culture as a whole that might be helpful: they are refugees, they have few belongings, they were once a dynasty, they are in the wilderness. They are nomadic. They are compared with the dung beetle.

Notice how deep these students are going—and they still don't have any claims, *let alone a thesis*.

Our next task is to organize the data. Sometimes the topic lends itself to natural breaks, as this one does with men, women, and children. We could also organize the data into symbols: the bell, the sheep and goat skins, and the coffee. We could then unpack the symbols; for example, in discussing the bell, some of my students have said the following:

It makes music.

It calls people to church (other contexts?). What is church? Worship, religion, structure, encounter, learning, gathering.

Bells are on clocks, ships.

What is a bell made of? Brass/metal. Strength. Gold? Silver? It shines, reflects light.

Is the shape relevant?

It echoes. Everyone can hear and feel it.

The boy is associated with the bell; thus, he is central to society.

Notice the amount of thought that is required to produce an engaging discussion. Essentially, we want to discover what world the author is evoking with a single word: *bell*.

Think about the questions that my students posed in their list and try to provide answers.

### *Make claims*

Now that we have collected and sorted our data, we must begin making claims—saying things about the data, inserting our own thoughts and language. Here are a few tips.

- Claims are not written directly in the text.
- Don't impose yourself on the text; try to detect your biases.
- Make sure none of the data in the text contradict your claims. You must be able to account for any contradictions.
- Quantity, not quality, is of essence at this stage.

Here are a few of my students' claims, which may or may not be verifiable. Some of the claims are fused with data—support from the text—which I've italicized.

Luxury is associated with this culture: *robe, richly woven carpet, embroidery.*

Women, in their hiddenness, bring strength to Bedouin culture.

Women do not have an identity; they are inferior.

Women are treasured: *they are associated with intricate stitching, and they hold the raw goods.*

*The boy calls to women with his voice and to men with his mortar:* he is the fulcrum of society.

The boy is a leader; he creates and brings change.

The men are the apex of the hierarchy.

Write three to five more claims about Bedouin culture.

### *Interpretation*

After gathering evidence and making claims, you can delve into investigation—constructing links between claims and support (the **I** in **CSI**). **I**'s should comprise approximately one-third of your essay, but often in student essays, I see instead reams and reams of data—too many quotations or long quotations with irrelevant details—or I see one claim after another with little support or investigation.

*A good essay has original thought.*

A good essay has original thought—and that's difficult to produce. If you find this step unchallenging, your claims are weak. Suppose, for example, that I've composed the following claim:

> There are strict lines of division between male and female roles in Bedouin society.

There is ample evidence to support this claim—women supply the raw goods while men consume the final product; women are shut off and men are visible. But I don't need to say anything else; I don't need to demonstrate that the **Cs** and **Ss** are linked; it's indisputable.

Consider, however, the following claim:

> The men's behaviour is instinctive.

This claim is far more intriguing; it requires support, and it invites the reader to step into the text and move around. I might provide the following evidence as support:

> The men respond to a bell-like sound—an echo.
> They all perform the same actions.
> They sit in a circle.

But more discussion is needed (**I**). I must explain why a circle or an action or an echo conveys something about instinct. The answer is not readily apparent—and significantly, there is room for the reader to disagree.

Here is one student's discussion about "Bedouin" with my comments in italics.

> Women in Arabic *[Avoid making generalizations; refer only to the people in the text: the Bedouin of 1891.]* culture are voiceless. The "Bedouin" excerpt shows that women were unheard throughout the morning coffee ritual—only the boy was heard as he made his small requests. These women, guarded behind the suspended wall, *[Very insightful.]* as ingredients for the coffee were supplied moments after requests were called out—yet no verbal response ever came. Either no words were needed, as the routine occurred daily, or words were not allowed

> to be spoken to a male, even to a young boy. When humans are denied access to their voice, they are denied access to expressing truth and connecting with others. *[Try not to generalize; remain inside the text by referring directly to the people in it. So the question is, can you prove this claim from the text? I think your idea of connecting with others is powerful. Can you make that your central claim (***C***) and elaborate on it?]* A family that values, honours, and respects each other chooses to hear other family members speak and voice ideas. *[Don't generalize; remain inside the text. Are you possibly imposing your own values on the text?]* Yet the women in "Bedouin" are silent. *[Your paragraph reflects the* **CSI** *method: good job.]*

I encouraged this student to make the following changes.

- Let your central claim (C) be that the women lack connection; your present claim, that they are voiceless, is not debatable. I cannot say, *Wrong! They certainly* do *have a voice*, because the text can't support such a claim; the women never speak (at least not within the confines of the text). Alternately, you could discuss the cause or effect of women's voicelessness, but this would be difficult to prove.
- Prove that the women lack connection. How do we connect? Speech and voice, touch, eye contact. What else?
- Finally, discuss the link between the evidence and the central claim (I). Could it be argued that the women are in fact connected through coffee making, that being invisible doesn't mean that they aren't connected? You said that they *listen*. Isn't that connectedness? I think we could debate this—so you have a good claim. Always anticipate the counter-argument to your claims; if you can't think of one, your claim is weak.

Here is the rewrite. The **claims** (C) are in bold, the *support* (S) in italics, and the investigation (I) is underlined.

> **Bedouin women in 1891 lacked connection**. The "Bedouin" excerpt shows that these *women were silent throughout the morning coffee ritual*. Guarded *behind the suspended wall*, they listened as ingredients for the coffee were called out—*yet no verbal response ever came*. Either no words were needed, as this routine occurred daily, or words were not allowed to be spoken. We all connect through conversation, which must include two parts: speaking and listening. If these women were denied access to their voice, they were denied communication—a necessary part of a relationship—with the boy and the men who received the coffee. Our own touch can create an unspoken language, an inner intimacy, that occurs when two bodies, hands or feet, embrace. *But when any kind of physical contact is shut off, like the women in the back of the embroidered hanging*, there is no chance to create or even experience closeness. We do not have to touch skin to show connection, but we must be near each other to establish the sense of belonging. *The robed men came to the fire to sit and have their coffee together, alongside the boy who served them. No words were exchanged, no one embraced, but they were among each other*. They breathed the same air in the presence of one another. Yet the women were never given the opportunity to commune with others, to sit and simply be present with them. Neither did the women have the chance for eye contact, *since the*

> *hanging created a barrier from touch and sight. The men and the boy never saw the women*—**as though it was purposeful to have disunion**. *No man put forth any word or act to display a desire for contact with the women.* **The women were disregarded; no bond was created**.

You may or may not agree with the assertions of this writer, and since this is a rough draft, she has some revisions to make. But the draft effectively employs the CSI method; the **claim** that women are disconnected (C) is supported by *evidence* from the text (S) and discussed at length (I).

The following sample shares the same views but does not support those views. I've bolded the claims that are not substantiated by the text.

> The Bedouin women experienced no bond with the men, nor were they exposed to the men. Each morning, the coffee was made to serve the men; the boy was diligent to give honour to them. He created a daily experience for them—an experience without the women. The women never tasted the coffee, never tasted the experience. They fell short of the honour of being served, because **the men were seen as worthier**. **The men perceived themselves as more valuable, and they let it be known**. The women were shut out, hidden behind the embroidered hanging, **not a choice but a deliberate direction, like a command they had to follow**. **The men neglected the women** and only sat near other men, **as the two opposites didn't hold equal worth**. The women were excluded, almost invisible, and only known by quick moments of an

> exposed hand. The hand appeared twice, unidentified. Maybe this hand belonged to different women, but what change would that make? **This was nothing but a hand that supplied coffee beans and cardamom seeds. Unknown to the served.**

This excerpt, unfortunately, takes leaps in logic. How do we know for certain that their lack of visibility designates the women as less worthy, less valuable, neglected, and subject to the commands of men? Division of labour, division of roles, does not necessarily denote a hierarchy of value. Therefore, I need to see a link between the claims and the evidence (the **I** in **CSI**).

The following writer offers a different view:

> In a brief review of the excerpt, it appears that the women in "Bedouin" are the lowest class of society: they remain out of sight and they do not speak. The very fact that they have a separate section in the tent supports this presupposition. But upon closer inspection, this argument comes apart. It's true that the women remain out of sight—yet they provide the resources needed for the boy to make coffee—they have the water and the cardamom that he needs to brew the pungent beverage. They are resourceful with supplies in their care and capable management. Their part of the tent is sectioned off with costly and intricately designed embroidered curtains. Embroidery is a work of art that takes time and expertise to create, with attention to detail that cannot be rushed: to think of these embroidered curtains in a nomadic camp indicates that the women are cared for and valued.

> The boy's role appears to be no more than to serve the older men; yet he is skilled and knowledgeable in his task, and evidently experienced in the art of coffee making. Fire tending is his responsibility, and such a large responsibility would not be entrusted to someone unworthy of it. For the Bedouins, there is no life without fire. That a child would be in charge of this duty reveals the confidence they have in younger ones being capable of fulfilling important roles.

To what extent does the writer effectively make claims, support them with evidence, and discuss the link between the claims and evidence? Notice that there is no link between arguments in this essay (the women and the boy); they could easily change places. In Takes Three and Four, we will review the Cut and Paste rule and discuss how to remedy this problem.

Write a **CSI** paragraph in response to one of your claims.

### *Integrating quotations*

Let's now discuss the difficult task of seamlessly integrating quotations into your own writing. Read the following excerpts and the comments that follow.

> Women seem to have a minimal role in this society; their section of the tent is voiceless: "he calls for water and coffee beans … the embroidered hanging that shuts off the women's section of the tent a hand passes them to him silently." This very subtle mention of women serving reflects different status in contrast to men; it is also critical

> to note that women assist the child in serving the men and elders.

This excerpt makes a claim, sets up the support with a colon, then adds a very short discussion. It would help if the writer described why service denotes a lower status ("**I**.").

If you reread the quotation, you'll notice that two words have been omitted and replaced by an ellipsis. However, the phrase is now ungrammatical because of the deleted words. The quotation should instead look like this: "he calls for water and for coffee beans, **and over** the embroidered hanging that shuts off the women's section of the tent a hand passes them to him silently." Ellipses are used to replace part of a sentence or paragraph that is irrelevant to your discussion. In this example, the writer might choose to say, "he calls for water and for coffee beans, **and over** the embroidered hanging…a hand passes them to him silently." Here, he is emphasizing the women's response to the boy's call.

It's sometimes difficult to know whether to use a direct or indirect quotation. In general, use a direct quotation when the language of the original text is important or powerful and you want to keep it intact. In the above example, the writer could add this:

> Later, "another hand—or is it the same one?—" passes seeds over the divider.

Here, I've used direct and indirect quotations. In the direct quotation, the author's original words and punctuation are so powerful that altering them would weaken the support. It is essential that you quote only the relevant parts of a text—and use ellipses to indicate that you have omitted part of the original.

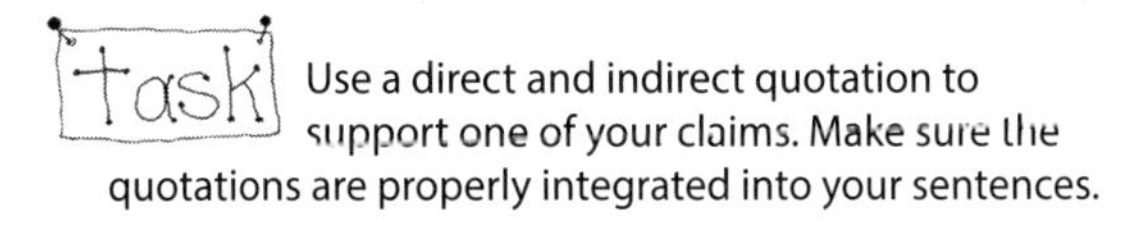

task
Use a direct and indirect quotation to support one of your claims. Make sure the quotations are properly integrated into your sentences.

## Step 3: Write a Thesis Statement

Once you've gathered data, created a number of claims, and discussed the link between the claims and support, you're ready to write a thesis statement—the central argument of your paper. The thesis is the answer to the question posed in the assignment; it's a super-claim, essentially, so it might come to the surface while you are generating individual claims.

*A thesis is essentially a super claim.*

The thesis statement is neither a statement of fact nor an observation; it *warrants* an essay and is usually debatable. Most writers place the thesis early in the essay—in the last sentence(s) of the introduction, or in longer essays, in the second paragraph—to establish their position and give readers a sense of their direction. Sometimes the thesis evolves and gains definition as you write; thus, the thesis of a rough draft is called a *working thesis*.

In writing a thesis, you must examine all of your **CSIs** and determine what they are saying to you. Essentially, you must bring them together under one umbrella—a thesis—and that is no easy task.

Here are several examples of thesis statements for "Bedouin" with a few observations.

Avoid thesis statements that are statements of fact and do not warrant an essay:

- The social structure of Bedouin society is divided into three groups: men, women, and children.
- Each person, be it man, woman or child, plays an important role through which they contribute to the well-being of the clan.

Avoid superficial thesis statements.

- The men and women in Robert Lacey's "Bedouin" are unforgettable characters.

Avoid thesis statements that go beyond the scope of the text or essay assignment.

- The itinerant Bedouin would one day establish a kingdom.

Avoid sentence structures such as *The point of my paper is...* or *In this essay, I will...*; they are wordy and self-evident.

- In this paper, I will discuss the relationship between men and women in Bedouin culture.

Be clear and specific; avoid vague language.

- There are advantages and disadvantages to the separation between men and women in Bedouin culture.

Rather dull theses, don't you think? Do you see yourself delving into these essays? The thesis statements are vague and noncommittal, as though the writers are afraid to say something. More significantly, they aren't debatable, so they don't warrant an essay.

But don't swing too far the other way; avoid making judgements that oversimplify complex issues and cannot be supported by the text, as in these examples:

- The men in Bedouin culture don't value women.
- The children are little more than slaves.
- The women in Bedouin culture are highly respected.

These thesis statements are difficult to prove because the text contains too much conflicting evidence. For example, if women are respected, why do they lack personal identity, why are they shut off, and why do they not share in the fruits of their labour? It's not that there shouldn't be any conflicting evidence—it's just that your thesis must be able to account for it. If that's creating difficulty, you need to reword it or toss it.

Here are a few superior thesis statements.

- The boy is the central figure around which Bedouin society revolves.
- Following prescribed gender roles creates harmony in Saudi society.
- Rituals allow the culture to thrive in harsh environments.
- Throughout exile, the Al Saud use expressions of servanthood to construct social boundaries.

These are compelling statements indeed; they require support (**S**) and interpretation (**I**). What is your view of the following thesis statement?

> The division between men and women in Bedouin culture ultimately allows displaced refugees to survive exile.

It might be difficult to demonstrate a causal relationship between gender division and the survival of Bedouin culture. Think of yourself as a lawyer—Nelson Mandela or Mahatma Gandhi or Amal Clooney. You must defend the thesis with claims and evidence drawn from the text. The wording of the thesis, then, is critical.

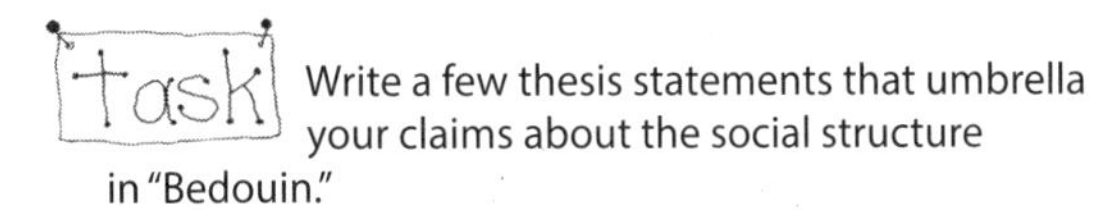

Write a few thesis statements that umbrella your claims about the social structure in "Bedouin."

## Step 4: Write the Introduction and Conclusion

Now that you've constructed your **CSIs** and thesis statement, you are ready to write the introduction and conclusion. Some students prefer to write the introduction first; others are frozen by the prospect of introducing something that doesn't exist—especially during an in-class exam—and write the introduction after completing a rough draft of the body. For your next essay assignment, try writing the introduction after drafting the body and see how it feels.

Please read the following introduction.

> In the excerpt "Bedouin," Robert Lacey weaves a brief yet rich Arabian history for his readers. The structure of Bedouin society is delicately and gently exposed. The structure is not clearly painted for the reader to observe, but it spreads out as the story unfolds. Boys serve men at the fire as they sit cross-legged on their sheep skin, while the women stay behind their embroidered divider, silent, but providing for all. Yet ultimately, it is the boy who is the central figure around which Bedouin societal structure revolves.

In the body of her essay, this writer uses the following arguments to support the thesis: the boy, through whom social structure and unity are created, controls the mortar, the ringing of the bell that calls people to action—and thus, he also controls the future. Very powerful. Notice that she doesn't "list" her claims in the thesis statement. Some professors prefer that students state the direction of their papers in the thesis; others deduct marks for what is called "excessive compression"—a mechanical or formulaic presentation that presses large ideas into a pithy phrase. If this writer wanted to reveal the direction of her paper within the thesis, she could say something like this:

> Yet it is the boy who is the central figure around which Bedouin societal structure revolves; his symbolic strike of the mortar calls for structure and community, and ultimately brings in the future.

In critical essays, the structure of the introduction is more rigid than it is in other types of papers. The first sentence typically states the title, author, and genre of the text(s) being analyzed and is followed by one or two sentences that outline the plot or central issues of the text(s). It is sometimes difficult to write in such a structured manner, so I recommend that you memorize a few samples. If you think canned sentences have no place in academic writing, consider this: mature writers have in their heads oodles of sentence structures to draw from. Why shouldn't you have a few of your own? Here are two examples.

> In the excerpt "Bedouin," Robert Lacey weaves a brief yet rich Arabian history for his readers.
>
> Robert Lacey's text "Bedouin" weaves a brief yet rich Arabian history for readers.

Now read the writer's conclusion.

> The boy strikes the brass mortar, evoking the ringing of a bell—a calling to the future, signifying that the boy *is* in fact the future of the Bedouin. Ultimately, the boy will become the man who is served. Sampling the coffee will no longer be enough; soon, he will enjoy the smooth

> drink as he leans back on his sheep skin—soothed by the aroma of the beans and the warmth of the fire. He will hold out his empty cup as a boy rushes over to refill it—he will waggle it from side to side. He has lived a full life, receiving provisions from the women and serving the men before him: now the future of the Bedouin society rests on his shoulders.

This conclusion beautifully exemplifies our Viva Puff. It sums up the essence of the arguments and points us to new thoughts, new ideas, that are *within the realm of the text*, connecting the ringing of the bell—a detail within the text—to the story beyond: the boy's future and ultimately the emergence of the Kingdom of Saudi Arabia. A good conclusion leaves us with something new to think about—but never moves outside of the text.

### Step 5: Write a Draft

You now have the pieces of your essay, and you must put them together into a draft. Your first task is to examine your CSIs and make sure that each one supports the thesis statement. Then, arrange them into a logical order, as we did with our smoking essay. It might be helpful at this point to write an outline to ensure that your ideas are linked before writing the draft.

Please read the following critique of "Bedouin" and answer the questions that follow. This student *owns* his writing; the ideas are his—they are not a concoction of the text. He has found his voice, and his writing is a joy to read. But there's room for improvement. As you read, think about how the essay can be refined.

## To Await a New Day

The scene set in the excerpt from "Bedouin" focusses on a single morning in a Nomadic camp. The richness of the imagery employed is marvelous, inviting the reader to delve deeply into the intricacies of Bedouin culture and social structure as demonstrated in the single action of a boy awakening the camp through the preparation of coffee. On an even deeper level though, the scene narrated here represents the rhythms of an exile expectancy for a greater future—a future which the same boy himself would come to initiate.

The sun slowly unfurls its warmth over the desert sand, a hand reaches from behind the fluttering barrier of a tent, the sound of coffee beans crushed against a brass mortar rings out for the camp to hear: all of this is the portends of one more day waiting. Although the scene smells of rote familiarity, the author gives indication that the lives of the characters painted in this scene were not always lived in itinerant wandering. Years were lined up like the hollow choir of the desert wind—each morning slowly eroding the memory of the walls that once surrounded the royal Al Sa'ud people. The boy whose preparation of coffee initiates the morning was only an infant when a rival dynasty forced their exile and bid them trade authority for a sheepskin saddle—wandering with the silent anonymity of the women hidden in their tent.

A semblance of regality might remain in the rich black of the goat haired tents, in the embroidery that grace the fluttering borders, and above all in the cross-legged gathering of the elders sipping coffee around the fire; but the luxuries allowed by the desert could not constitute a desirable future. Like the camels "irked by the thong's that hobble their forelegs," the boy's morning ritual was one permeated by waiting—waiting for water to warm, for the first crack of roasted beans, and for the men to finally drink the last of the exile wandering that defined them.

**Questions**

1. As noted in Step 5, the introduction to a literary analysis should include the following:
   - a sentence stating the title, author, and genre of the text;
   - one or more sentences that outline the plot or relevant themes of the text; and
   - a clear, debatable thesis.

   Does the introduction meet these requirements?
2. Does the body of the essay follow our **CSI** method? Find examples to support your claim.
3. Does this essay follow our Cut and Paste rule? In other words, are there sentences or paragraphs that can be moved to a new location without significantly altering the essay?
4. An effective conclusion reminds the reader of the thesis without duplicating the introduction or reiterating the claims of the essay. Is this an effective conclusion? Why or why not?
5. A good essay is essentially a good read. Did you enjoy reading this essay?

6. This assignment requested a 500-word response, but the essay is only 334 words. How could the writer have extended his arguments without impairing the essay?

## Editorial Eye

Part of writing an excellent essay is proofreading your drafts—paying close attention to word choice, sentence structure, and mechanics. Upon close review, you might find that although your words and sentences sound good, they disguise a poor argument, make a vague or meaningless assertion, or hide a lack of clarity in your thinking. Polish your work with a slow, careful, and critical review before handing it in. Let's examine the student essay we just analyzed—"To Await a New Day"—this time looking at the details, not the overall argument.

### To Await a New Day

The scene set in the excerpt from "Bedouin" focusses on a single morning in a Nomadic camp. The richness of the imagery employed is marvelous, inviting the reader to delve deeply into the intricacies of Bedouin culture and social structure as demonstrated in the single action of a boy awakening the camp through the preparation of coffee. On an even deeper level though, the scene narrated here represents the rhythms of an exile expectancy for a greater future—a future which the same boy himself would come to initiate.

There's no need to capitalize "Nomadic" because it is not a proper noun. Consult a dictionary when you are unsure about capitalization.

Consider rewriting this to say, "The richness of the imagery invites the reader to delve..." This shows us more specifically how the imagery is "marvelous."

I'm not sure what this means. Could it say, "the rhythms of a people in exile, a people in expectancy, waiting for a greater future"?

The sun slowly unfurls its warmth over the desert sand, a hand reaches from behind the fluttering barrier of a tent, the sound of coffee beans crushed against a brass mortar rings out for the camp to hear: all of this is the portends of one more day waiting. Although the scene smells of rote familiarity, the author gives indication that the lives of the characters painted in this scene were not always lived in itinerant wandering. Years were lined up like the hollow choir of the desert wind—each morning slowly eroding the memory of the walls that once surrounded the royal Al Sa'ud people. The boy whose preparation of coffee initiates the morning was only an infant when a rival dynasty forced their exile and bid them trade authority for a sheepskin saddle—wandering with the silent anonymity of the women hidden in their tent.

Check your word choice; "portend" is a verb, not a noun. So you might say, "all of this portends one more day waiting." Or perhaps you want "portent," which is a noun meaning an omen: "all of this is the portent of one more day waiting."

A semblance of regality might remain in the rich black of the goat haired tents, in the embroidery that graced the fluttering borders, and above all in the cross-legged gathering of the elders sipping coffee around the fire; but the luxuries allowed by the desert could not constitute a desirable future. Like the camels "irked by the thong's that hobble their forelegs," the boy's morning ritual was one permeated by waiting—waiting for water to warm, for the first crack of roasted beans, and for the men to finally drink the last of the exile wandering that defined them.

Should be "grace." It's a convention to write about literature in the present tense.

Proofread carefully. You're using a possessive, not a plural here (inserting an error and not quoting the original accurately).

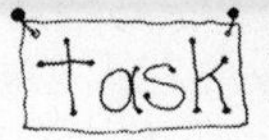


Write your own essay in response to our "Bedouin" question: *Describe the social structure of Bedouin society in 1891* (see Appendix 1 for the text).

Focus on the following principles:

1. Writing process
2. Understanding the question
3. CSI
4. Integrating quotations
5. Debatable thesis
6. Cut and Paste rule
7. Bleeding paragraphs
8. Natural and artificial transitions
9. Lopsided essays
10. Introduction and conclusion

# *TAKE THREE*

We will now move from Saudi Arabia to Morocco and loop through the essay-writing process again with a slightly more difficult text, George Orwell's essay "Marrakech" (see Appendix 2, page 188, for the full text). The guidelines in this section apply not only to critical essays, but to all theoretical essay assignments.

I'll give you another straightforward essay question: *What does George Orwell's essay "Marrakech" convey about colonialism?*

8

# Integrating and Discussing Quotations

At the crux of essay writing is grappling with ideas—yours and others'. To a large extent, then, you are deciphering quotations, embedding them in your piece, and saying something intelligible about them. Thus, I cannot overemphasize the importance of using sources properly and, by extension, of using the CSI method.

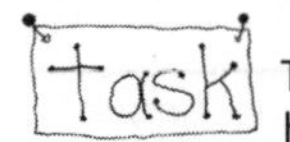


The following task should take you a few hours to complete.

First, reread our essay question to ensure that you understand it. Then read "Marrakech" a few times (see Appendix 2), highlighting every detail that is relevant to colonialism. Next, use the **CSI** method to do the following:

- collect all data in the text that is related to colonialism (**S**);
- cut and paste similar ideas together;
- make claims about colonialism based on the data (**C**);
- discuss the relationship between each claim and its supporting data (**I**).

You should now be sitting before a mound of **CSI**s. Thus, you are in a better position to scrutinize other students' work. Please read the following analyses of "Marrakech" and correct your own **CSI**s if you see similar errors.

(Please note that in this book, we do not discuss the rules of Chicago, MLA, APA, or other academic citation formats. Formatting is a matter of following simple rules, and you can go directly to the relevant websites or to your own institution's library website for that information.)

## Make Sure Your Claims Are Debatable

This writer chooses effective quotations to support his claims (although he uses too many), but the claims aren't debatable. After reading Orwell's piece, do I need to be convinced that oppression and poverty exist in Marrakech?

> One central theme across this essay is the prevalence of war-initiated poverty and the impact that it has on the oppressed. Immediately, Orwell paints images of poverty through statements such as "When you walk through a town like this—two hundred thousand inhabitants, of whom at least twenty thousand own literally nothing except the rags they stand up in." Perhaps the most powerful evidence of poverty is the Arab navy's request of Orwell's bread, which is intended for the gazelle: "He looked from the gazelle to the bread and from the bread to the gazelle, with a sort of quiet amazement, as though he had never seen anything quite like this before." In tangent with lack of material goods is a message of the Spanish war; death throughout the city: "The burying-ground is merely a huge waste of hummocky earth, like a derelict building-lot. After a month or two no one can even be certain where his own relatives are buried." Orwell makes it clear that the city is completely impoverished with both death and lack of material goods due to a war that it has been drawn into by colonial rulers.

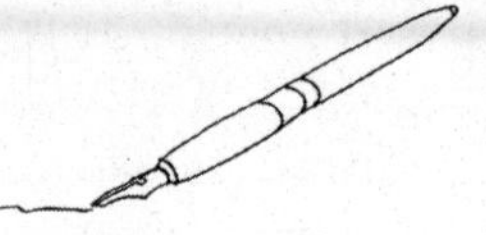

## Editorial Eye

This piece can also use a close review of the details. See below for comments an editor might make to improve the writing.

One central theme across this essay is the prevalence of war-initiated poverty and the impact that it has on the oppressed. Immediately, Orwell paints images of poverty through statements such as, "When you walk through a town like this—two hundred thousand inhabitants, of whom at least twenty thousand own literally nothing except the rags they stand up in." Perhaps the most powerful evidence of poverty is the Arab navy's request of Orwell's bread, which is intended for the gazelle: "He looked from the gazelle to the bread and from the bread to the gazelle, with a sort of quiet amazement, as though he had never seen anything quite like this before." In tangent with lack of material goods is a message of the Spanish war; death throughout the city: "The burying-ground is merely a huge waste of hummocky earth, like a derelict building-lot. After a month or two no one can even be certain where his own relatives are buried."

**Consider reducing this quotation to "...by describing a town of 'two hundred thousand inhabitants, of whom at least twenty thousand own literally nothing except the rags they stand up in.'" Include only the part of the sentence that supports the argument that Orwell is painting scenes of poverty.**

**Watch your word choice. Orwell describes a "navvy"—a road or canal labourer, not a "navy"—a nation's ships of war.**

**"request of Orwell's bread" might sound like he is asking the bread for something. Rephrase this to "request for Orwell's bread."**

**Semicolons connect independent clauses (or complete sentences). Rephrase this sentence so that each part (before and after the semicolon) can stand alone.**

> Orwell makes it clear that the city is completely impoverished with both death and lack of material goods due to a war that it has been drawn into by colonial rulers.

---

## Integrate Quotations with Your Own Writing

When you use quotations, they should read as though they were part of your own writing; they should be seamlessly integrated, as in the following example. This student chooses quotations aptly and includes only the parts that support her claim.

> He carries on with the air of unveiled objectivity, turning the reader's gaze to the weary faces of overlooked old women "mummified with age and the sun," to the slumped countenance of the Negro army marching like "a flock of cattle," and to the tightly packed Jewish children who fill the streets in "unbelievable numbers, like clouds of flies." The characters exist in a state that none would deem worthy of humanity, yet they remain altogether overlooked by the collective European conscience.

## Avoid Summarizing Quotations

In the following excerpt, the writer has a strong sense of the art and rhythm of sentences and integrates quotations seamlessly. But to some extent, he summarizes Orwell's position and essentially makes the same argument: that colonialism renders people invisible.

> Invisibility, for Orwell, is the informant of the absurdity he elucidates, and this, surrounded by imagery and analogy, is driven home by his personal point of view

which stands as the representative of European society as a whole. In one striking example, he informs the reader of his own indignation over the brutal treatment of animals, which surfaced far more readily than remorse over human suffering, so quickly overlooked. Rather than perceiving humans as crushed beneath the weight of loads too great for their frail backs, he saw firewood passing: "Yet I suppose I had not been five minutes on Moroccan soil before I noticed the overloading of the donkeys and was infuriated by it." It is ridiculous to him that one could be so oblivious to the suffering of human beings when a mere difference in skin colour and geography would enrage us. "No one would think of running cheap trips to the Distressed Areas. But where the human beings have brown skin their poverty is simply not noticed." They blend in, he argues, to the dirt they scrape their living from while the European gaze is set upon the wealth they can acquire at their expense. Not only are the people unnoticed, they are not worth noticing. Orwell asks, "Are they really the same flesh as yourself? Do they even have names?" The reality he postulates in response is the trampling of skeletons underfoot in shallow graves without marking or memorial. To the European, they are but a faceless addition to the landscape, hardly to be considered on equal footing with the white form looming above them.

## Avoid Using Too Many Quotations

**In the next example, quotations form too much of the discussion.**

> Oppression towards the Jews is deafening within this text, everything from the old men rushing at an opportunity to get a cigarette, to the grandfather and his grandson: "thanks to a lifetime of sitting in this position his left leg is warped out of shape. At his side his grandson, aged six, is already starting on the simpler parts of the job." Not only are Jews oppressed; so are work animals: "It is usual to plough with a cow and a donkey yoked together. Two donkeys would not be quite strong enough, but on the other hand two cows would cost a little more to feed." Of course, it would be optimal for the farmers to use two cows, but due to the poverty, they have no other choice but to unequally yoke the donkey with the cow, a sign of necessary cruelty and inefficacy. "After a dozen years of devoted work it suddenly drops dead, whereupon its master tips it into a ditch and the village dogs have torn its guts out before its cold."

It's difficult to resist the inclination to lean on the text, but think of your essay as a building under construction. Quotations are the scaffolds that provide support, not the building itself. Yet in many essays, quotations make up the entire building, and the writer's ideas are mere scaffolding—if they are present at all. Try to reverse that scenario. Take the time to conduct in-depth research and mull over your ideas.

## Include Your Own Ideas

The next example ends with a powerful claim, and if the writer had discussed some of her own ideas relevant to the claim (**I**), the argument would be outstanding.

> However, each one of these people groups *struggled* in slightly different ways. They all struggled with being shunned as a lower class of human being, but in practice, it *looks* a little different. The colonists in the first section *have driven* the people into nothingness, not allowing them to survive in the land they called home. The Arab had a job but was not paid a livable wage. The Jews were allowed to have a community in the city but squished into tiny sections. Thousands of Jews expected to live in a city without a way of obtaining proper resources. The Moroccans' land was decimated: with no trees to keep moisture, the land turned to rock. They could not continue to live and grow in the patterns of life they *have always known*. The soldiers were poorly dressed and treated as if their lives didn't matter. Thousands of them, all with rifles: being commanded by handfuls of white men. Orwell deliberately took issues that looked slightly different to show us something. There is not a cookie cutter answer to the problem; oppression *takes* many forms. The way in which the white man *has taken* control *was* shaped to the environment they went to.

Notice the shifts between verb tenses (I italicized a few examples). It's preferable to use the present tense in a literary analysis, but more important is that the tense be consistent.

## Don't Impose on the Text

So then. You need I's. But how to produce them? First, don't impose on the text; don't pull it beyond its limits, as this writer does.

> Western readers will quickly extract the theme of invisibility from the text, chaff at how Orwell outlines the invisibility of poor people, and assume responsibility for the invisibility, blaming white supremacy. But that isn't Orwell's objective; he says, "I write it because there is some lie that I want to expose, some fact to which I want to draw attention, and my initial concern is to get a hearing." His intent is to show how much misuse is in their social system, how disrespect and degradation by their own people contribute to the cycle of poverty that they can't escape—they are invisible to their own people. It isn't white people's abuse that has put them where they are; instead, it's the injurious treatment by their own people, those in close circles who have reduced them to, as Orwell describes, "poor old earth-coloured bodies, bodies reduced to bones and leathery skin."

This writer is *saying* something, making the debatable claim that invisibility is at least partially self-inflicted in Marrakech. But be careful about word choice. Is Orwell's piece about white supremacy or colonialism?

Also, avoid making claims about an author's purpose or objective: it's difficult to know these things unless the author explicitly states his intent or unless you frequently visit his home for Friday evening board games. In this example, Orwell does in fact state his purposes for writing—but has this student correctly interpreted his words? Does the quotation specify that the "lie" concerns disrespect for and degradation of the Moroccan people? This writer imposes her own version of Orwell's intent on the text. Notice, however, that the quotations in this excerpt read as though they were part of the student's own writing—an excellent execution indeed.

## Use Appropriate Language

In some ways, I enjoy the following piece because the writer *owns* his arguments; the references to the text are scaffolds supporting his claim that oppression is situational—a compelling proposition to ponder. The paragraph is also seamless: not a single sentence can be cut and pasted. This writer has my attention, and I anticipate reading his investigation (I).

> Often times when we are presented with an issue by a single person, there is a thought that crosses all our minds at some point. *What did this person do to get themselves into this mess*? Then someone else shares the same issue, and you start thinking, *Maybe there is something wrong*, but you don't want it to bother you yet. Later, you hear someone else share the same struggles and the same trials as the two before. Now it starts to click, and soon enough, there are hundreds of people presenting this issue and you can't ignore it anymore. You realize that it isn't just one person's mistake. There is a greater issue that you never realized. There is a saying around here: *It takes three car accidents to get traffic lights installed*. In the same way, George Orwell uses this technique in his essay. At first, we are given a single glimpse into the lives of a community that is impoverished beyond anything you could imagine. You start to get emotionally attached and wonder about the big question, *What has happened here*? Given the answer that it is the "white man" and the Colonial institution, you think, *They were probably like this before anyways*. However, you then get a glimpse of another community, with the Arab navvy. His life is broken, too: not by

> anything he has done. After that, the Jewish Ghettos, the Moroccan people struggling to survive on their scorched land, and the army of brainwashed soldiers who think that they are merely the tools that the white man controls. After all this, it is impossible to believe that the issue is their own doing. Something, someone, came and did this to these people. George Orwell had to use these broken segments of pain and sorrow in order to show us that it was not just one person's poor decision to ruin their life. He had to use these multiple events to show that there was a greater issue.

Unfortunately, this writing is far too colloquial. The writer takes too long to introduce the text (this is only a four-page essay), and he uses the second-person point of view (*you*), which should be avoided in academic essays. The initial sentences, if written more concisely, could be effective in an introduction, but they shouldn't appear in the body, whose purpose is to analyze the *text*, not to describe the inner life of the reader.

The paragraph does, in fact, read like an introduction; it transitions well between the preamble and Orwell and ends with a hint about what the controlling idea of the essay will be. I see this often: introductory sentences misplaced in the body. This is the reason that many writers prefer to write the introduction after writing the body.

## Do It Well

The following excerpt, I think, is a beautiful example of CSI.

> Insects fly through the vibrant streets and marketplaces, around the sweet smell of pomegranate and the delicate pottery. They live immersed in simple beauty, but that

> holds no power over the flies: they are small and brown and ugly. People do not walk to the market to view flies because they contain no attraction, no wonder, no awe. Who partakes of the energetic market to buy fresh fruit and instead stares at brown flies? The brown people in the excerpt—small, poor, and ugly—contrast with the beautiful land they live in. These people blend in just as the land stands out. Travellers come to witness the beauty that the land holds; they desire to see it for themselves. The tourists are unaware that the most beautiful land consists of the poorest people, and maybe they never become conscious of the contrast. Maybe they only see what they choose to—beauty.

I like the way this writer juxtaposes details in the text. In repeating the words *small*, *brown*, *ugly*, she draws a parallel between flies and people without spelling it out and insulting my intelligence. There is evidence of **CSIs** in her discussion, and they are so tightly woven that I'm not distracted by artificial structures; rather, I'm thinking about what beauty is, what compels us, and how our humanity becomes debased. Great essays like this one leave openings for the reader to offer a counter-signature, as Derrida puts it—to enter in and move around.

**Choose two or three examples of CSI paragraphs in this section and rewrite them.**

# 9

# Transitions

Once we've delineated our arguments in a series of CSI paragraphs, how do we put them together in the form of a Viva Puff, not an Oreo? How do we order our arguments so the essay is seamless? My suggestion: put similar ideas together using natural transitions to draw logical connections.

Consider the following discussion about "Marrakech."

> **Last sentences of argument 1**: He performs back-breaking labour, wears nothing but rags and begs for food. He answers to those in authority who use him to further their agenda.
>
> **First sentences of argument 2**: Orwell includes details that the people don't even notice as they walk down their streets. They don't notice the river of urine, or the young boy who is working alongside his grandfather. They cannot see the stooped old women under her load of firewood or the young man who was taken from everything familiar and placed into the army to advance the agenda of those in power.

While I love the use of detail to support the claims, I don't see a clear link between the idea of authority in the first paragraph and invisibility in the second. Notice, however, that both excerpts state that the powerful use the poor to advance their agendas, so this idea could perhaps be used as a link, a natural transition between paragraphs.

In the following essay, the writer discusses people's irrelevance in "Marrakech." She is attempting to create natural transitions between paragraphs by threading ideas together. The transitions still feel a little contrived, but with practice, she'll soon be writing a seamless essay. Her artificial transition in Argument 2—*The second purpose of the earth is to*—is, I hope you'll agree, wordy and conspicuous.

### Argument 1

Orwell begins by speaking about a corpse and the clouds of flies that are following it, instantly triggering thoughts of death in the minds of his readers. He's talking about a Moroccan funeral, and how insubstantial the life is. The only people who mourn the lost lives are the males. It's almost as if he is telling his readers that the females know that the purpose of life is death. He shows how the camels are used to death and that they've developed a chant to wail along with the funeral procession. Since death is the Moroccans' purpose, no attention is given to life. Bodies aren't prepared for burial—except for an insignificant rag wrapped around the body—and they are dumped into the shallow graves as if they're as unimportant as waste. The Moroccans aren't given a gravestone or name to mark the importance that their life once was: they've accomplished death, and their lives will not be remembered. No effort or time is given to digging their grave and no coffin is given for the protection of their bodies from **earth's** decay.

## Argument 2

The **earth** has a few purposes. One is to provide toil and struggle to the Moroccan people: it's a constant reminder of the impending death waiting at their door. The labour that the earth demands advances the death of the people. The work of the land is mostly done by hand, crippling the body and bringing about aches and pains that only death will cure. The relentless work brings about meagre crops, reminding the Moroccans of possible starvation and death; their purpose is merely death, not to work the land. The second purpose of the earth is to aid in the decomposition and decay of life itself. The Moroccans' decomposition and decay produces the soil and earth that the others will toil with and be buried in. Orwell tells his readers that just as a life is risen from the earth, after sweating and starving for years, they are returned to earth in their unmarked graves, like **donkeys** kicked to the ditch at the end of their time.

## Argument 3

The lives of Moroccan people are as irrelevant as a **donkey's**. The donkey is a willing and faithful worker, like the Moroccans; it carries more than one would think is possible. After all its years of devoted work, the donkey dies and is tossed into the ditch—cast aside like garbage—for the animals to feast upon and aid in the decomposition process. The donkey succeeded in death: it lived its toilsome life for the same purpose as the Moroccans—death. The donkey is known as a beast of burden, the same name given to the **old women** of Marrakech.

### Argument 4

The **old women** of Marrakech are described as being mummified, bringing images of death and decay. The older women are described as death before they've even passed on. They're shrinking and shriveling and have bodies of bones and leathery skin: they are decaying before the reader's eyes. Orwell describes an older lady wailing in response to him. The reader is brought back to the wailing camels during the funeral at the beginning of the text, chanting and mourning an inevitable death—one's sole purpose.

Have you ever participated in a triathlon—a race with swimming, cycling, and running? I haven't. Nor do I want to. But I've heard that the most important part of the race is the transitions—the links between events that can make or break a race. Transitions are called the fourth discipline of triathlon, and I would use the same terminology to describe essay writing: transitions are a fine-tuning of the essay that reveal a higher level of discipline and critical thinking.

# 10

# Introductions and Conclusions

After completing a draft of the body, you are ready to write the introduction and conclusion—a difficult task, indeed. Let's examine a few student samples.

### Introduction

Here, there, and everywhere—yet nowhere. This is the message poured out by George Orwell in his essay "Marrakech." Throughout his essay, we are shown how the trials of many different people groups are caused by a single entity—the White man. The use of different people groups in different scenarios is an effective way to present this issue as the only thing that matters. At the end of the essay, it has become the only issue that matters, or even the only issue that has ever really truly mattered.

### Conclusion

It was not a mistake for George Orwell to use many different scenarios. In fact, it has only enforced his essay's

> point. Throughout it, we get so emotionally attached to these people. The use of fragmented passages leaves us with an issue that makes us believe that the oppression caused by overbearing, unrighteous, power hungry rulers is the only issue that has ever truly mattered.

This introduction is properly structured: it mentions the title, author, and genre of the text in the first sentences, provides a short synopsis, then states the thesis. Similarly, the conclusion reminds us of the thesis and makes a few interesting comments—although it is somewhat tedious because it repeats parts of the introduction verbatim. However, I'm not entirely sure of what idea this essay is trying to develop. The thesis—and consequently, the essay—isn't debatable or compelling because it doesn't make a clear assertion. In Take Four, we'll revisit this idea of writing powerful introductions and conclusions.

**Rewrite the thesis statement in the above introduction.**

# 11

# Examining a Draft

Please read the following essay and answer the questions that follow.

## Colonialism in Orwell's "Marrakech"

George Orwell, in his work *Marrakech*, seeks to bring to the foreground the absurd cruelty of colonial power through the elucidation of the human experience within such societal structures. It is his argument that all colonial empires are founded upon the ideal of human worthlessness, and in the case of European power, the worthlessness of those who are brown skinned. Once a people can be deemed less than human and maintained in such a state by the perceived supremacy of the oppressors, they are enabled to become exploited with a level of injustice that defies all sense of morality.

Readily apparent from the start of the excerpt is the powerful use of imagery, which in many ways is the linchpin of Orwell's argument. The reader is dropped into the streets of Colonial Morocco with the immediate apprehension of flies, filth, and the corpses of those who live and breathe their last submerged in the stench of it all. It is by detailing the conditions of the place and the lives of the people within it that the absurdity of it all is tasted with the greatest repugnance. He carries on with the air of unveiled objectivity; turning the reader's gaze to the weary faces of overlooked old women, "mummified with age and the sun," to the slumped countenance of the Negro army marching like "a flock of cattle," and to the tightly packed Jewish children who fill the streets in "unbelievable numbers, like clouds of flies." It is not debatable that the characters seem to exist in a state none would deem worthy of humanity; and yet they remain altogether overlooked by the collective European conscience: Orwell says, "I am not commenting, merely pointing to the fact."

Orwell uses the flies as an apt analogy to the weary people on display—sifting through the rags and soil, crowding like swarms around the urine-soaked streets in gasps of life before dying with the same meaning to society as those companions of carrion. They are overpacked and overworked; their only concern the ongoing struggle to survive in an environment that is hostile and unconcerned for them; unconcerned, that is, aside for the times when they like flies become an annoyance and the objects of attack. This Orwell highlights as being well known by the Jews especially, who are burdened with insult added to degrading injury in the accusation that they control all of the world's wealth to profit at its expense. In light of the subhuman conditions observed it is simply comical that such an accusation would be leveled unless the accuser were blind or the state of the accused were invisible.

Invisibility, for Orwell, is the informant of the absurdity he elucidates, and this, surrounded by imagery and analogy, is driven home by his personal point of view which stands as the representative of European society as a whole. In one striking example, he informs the reader of his own indignation of the brutal treatment of animals as something which surfaced far more readily than the human suffering so quickly overlooked. Rather than perceiving humans crushed beneath the weight of loads too great for their frail backs he saw "firewood passing." "Yet I suppose I had not been five minutes on Moroccan soil before I noticed the overloading of the donkeys and was infuriated by it." It is ridiculous to him that one could be so oblivious to the suffering of human beings when a mere difference in skin colour and geography would enrage us. "No one would think of running cheap trips to the Distressed Areas. But where the human beings have brown skin their poverty is simply not noticed." They blend in, he argues, to the dirt they scrape their living upon while the European gaze is set upon the wealth they can acquire at their expense. Not only are the people unnoticed they are not worth noticing. Orwell asks, "Are they really the same flesh as yourself? Do they even have names?" The reality he postulates in response is the irregular trampling of skeletons underfoot in shallow graves without marking or memorial. To the European they are but a faceless addition to the landscape, hardly to be considered on equal footing with the white form looming above them.

What is made abundantly clear in this work is that even the most absurd of abuse, the most putrid of environments, and the most demeaning societal structures can be justified when the inhabitants crushed by these things are no longer seen as human. A fly may be swatted without a second thought to its value, and in equal measure, an entire people can be trodden upon without any significant moral qualm. Using imagery, analogy and the elucidation of personal perspective, George Orwell conveys with brutal clarity the fact that beneath the facade of empirical glory lies the twisted absurdity of human life reduced to the movement of flies swarming over a restaurant table.

**Questions**

1. **Let's break down the thesis statement: *Once a people can be deemed less than human and maintained in such a state by the perceived supremacy of the oppressors, they are enabled to become exploited with a level of injustice that defies all sense of morality.***

**Try not to besiege your thesis with a plethora of superfluity. Wordiness *sounds* intelligent, but if your**

professor has to reread the thesis several times to discern its intent, she'll be exhausted before she reaches the depths of your arguments. The thesis essentially says this: *exploitation occurs when oppressors deem that a people group is less than human.* This essay, then, must prove two things: that the colonizers in Marrakech deem the people to be less than human and that this perspective *causes* the exploitation in Marrakech.

It's important to break down your thesis in this way to determine whether your essay achieves its purpose: to prove the thesis. There is no doubt that both suffering and exploitation occur in Marrakech; the question is, does one cause the other and, specifically, does that causal relationship occur because one group deems the other to be less than human?

Examine this essay paragraph by paragraph, sentence by sentence, and determine whether or not the thesis is successful.

2. What are the central claims in the essay? Does the evidence in each paragraph support the claims? Do quotations or the writer's own ideas serve as scaffolding?
3. Does this essay follow our Cut and Paste rule? Are there sentences or paragraphs that can be moved without significantly altering the essay?
4. To what extent does the writer own the essay? That is, can you discern the writer's voice?
5. As I mentioned earlier, a good essay is essentially a good read. Did you enjoy reading this essay?

## Editorial Eye

As noted in question 1 above, this writer clearly enjoys the sound of language, but perhaps takes it too far at times, creating insubstantial phrases and sentences. Always check your work, and try to delineate your arguments as concisely as possible.

> George Orwell, in his work *Marrakech*, seeks to bring to the foreground the absurd cruelty of colonial power through the elucidation of the human experience within such societal structures. It is his argument that all colonial empires are founded upon the ideal of human worthlessness, and in the case of European power, the worthlessness of those who are brown skinned. Once a people can be deemed less than human and maintained in such a state by the perceived supremacy of the oppressors, they are enabled to become exploited with a level of injustice that defies all sense of morality.
>
> Readily apparent from the start of the excerpt is the powerful use of imagery, which in many ways is the linchpin of Orwell's argument.

Book titles are shown in italics, but titles of poems, essays, or book chapters are shown in quotation marks. This should be "Marrakech."

Your essay assignment will likely limit the number of words you can use, so try not to waste words that could otherwise be used to deepen your discussion. Could this phrase perhaps say, "George Orwell, in his work *Marrakech*, reveals the cruelty of colonial power. . ."? The second part of the sentence is more difficult to edit, because an "elucidation of the human experience within . . . societal structures" is essentially what most literary texts do. Think about what you want to say and try to convey your ideas as concisely as possible. See my book *Cut It Out* to learn how to write concisely.

Why not use "He argues"? Two words instead of four.

Be careful of word choice. An "ideal" is the perception of what is perfect. Is that what you mean, or is it just the *idea* of human worthlessness? But really, it's just some humans that are considered worthless, not all.

Revise to "become exploited" and cut three words.

A slow start up for this sentence. Does "Readily apparent from the start of the excerpt" add anything to the argument? Why not leap right into what you want to say with "Orwell's powerful imagery is the linchpin of his argument." In this way, you highlight your own powerful image: "linchpin."

The reader is dropped into the streets of Colonial Morocco with the immediate apprehension of flies, filth, and the corpses of those who live and breathe their last submerged in the stench of it all. It is by detailing the conditions of the place and the lives of the people within it that the absurdity of it all is tasted with the greatest repugnance. He carries on with the air of unveiled objectivity; turning the reader's gaze to the weary faces of overlooked old women, "mummified with age and the sun," to the slumped countenance of the Negro army marching like "a flock of cattle," and to the tightly packed Jewish children who fill the streets in "unbelievable numbers, like clouds of flies." It is not debatable that the characters seem to exist in a state none would deem worthy of humanity; and yet they remain altogether overlooked by the collective European conscience: Orwell says, "I am not commenting, merely pointing to the fact."

> No capitalization needed. It should be "colonial Morocco."

> The "meat" of your sentence begins with "the characters," so why not begin there?

> Be careful when you state what "everyone" or "no one" thinks or believes. Try reworking this sentence to read, "The characters seem to exist in a sub-human state..."

---

**task** Write your own essay in response to the "Marrakech" question: What does George Orwell's essay "Marrakech" convey about colonialism?

Focus on the following principles:

1. **CSI**
2. Integrating and discussing quotations
3. Transitioning between arguments
4. Cut and paste rule
5. Bleeding paragraphs
6. Debatable thesis
7. Introduction and conclusion
8. Writer's voice

# *TAKE FOUR*

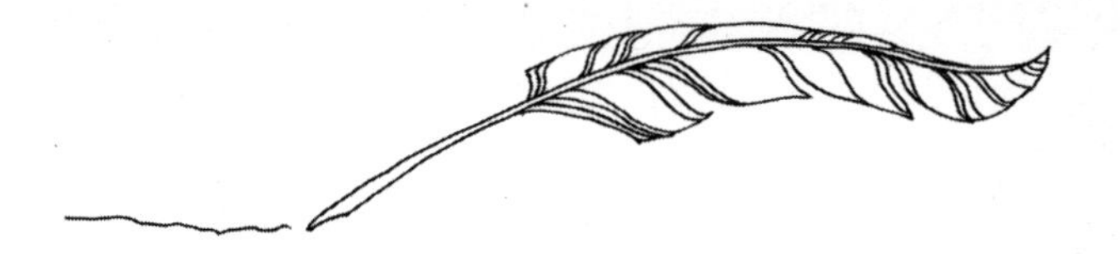

I hope that you now have a solid understanding of the essay-writing process, CSI, thesis, and essay structure. Let's now scrutinize some longer excerpts that discuss social issues rather than literary texts. We will apply the lessons learned here to the essay you wrote about "Marrakech" in Take Three.

## 12

# Primary and Secondary Sources

In most essay assignments, you will be asked to support your arguments with primary and/or secondary sources. Primary sources are original documents and firsthand accounts of events; examples include photographs, audio/video recordings, films,

*Use both primary and secondary sources to support your arguments.*

journals, letters, speeches, diaries, newspaper articles, interviews, and artifacts. Many students avoid using primary sources, perhaps because they don't fully understand their import. Yet conducting your own research, rather than reporting exclusively on others', fortifies and freshens your paper. Try interviewing someone who has direct experience with your topic; your writing will be *real* because it is birthed in a personal encounter.

Secondary sources form the bulk of student research; they are written by someone else after an event has occurred or by someone who has examined a primary source. They consist of information that researchers have gathered, interpreted, and recorded in books, articles, and other publications. Secondary sources are extremely important in validating and substantiating your arguments—but remember, this is *your* paper, *your* thesis.

As you read the following excerpts from undergraduate student essays, consider how the writers unpack quotations and integrate other writers' words with their own. Which excerpts do you think most effectively use sources to support an argument? Please note that the excerpts are rough drafts, and some contain numerous errors. All excerpts could use more work, but we'll examine some common mistakes with our "Editorial Eye."

## Use Current and Relevant Sources

The following writer's sources are quite dated—some over forty years old. Over time, views change, science changes, and language changes. Some of the ideas in this paper seem archaic, and I'm wondering whether the thesis would be different had the writer used current sources.

### On Being "Normal"

Stigmatization extends to race, gender, and religious ideologies—to anything or anyone who is different from what we consider "normal." Many sociologists have concluded that the problem revolves around how disabilities have been sociologically defined. Disabled people are, as Abberley (1993) points out, often "only relevant as problems" and are "thus excluded from the making of the cultural, political, and intellectual world. 'Problem' is the definition of the situation of disability" (Thomas, 1971). Disability is considered to be a problem in society, an inconvenience, something that "normal" people need to work around in order to accommodate themselves and the disabled. As Titchkosky (2000) states,

> Such an understanding does not arise simply because our bodies give us troubles; disability as a problem is presented to people through interaction with the social and physical environment, and through the social production of knowledge. (p. 198)

If disability isn't managed or taken care of, it becomes a destructive part of life, blemishing society; it becomes a form of deviance in society if it is not controlled (Tichkosky, 2000, p. 206). Thus, disability is defined sociologically not only as a problem, but as a problem that must be managed, and the disabled person in this view becomes someone who needs to be managed or fixed, someone who must cope or hide: "Sociological investigation has focussed almost entirely upon the stigmatized or marked individuals as passive recipients of the mark and its accompanying stereotype and upon the management techniques that marked individuals use to cope with their burden" (Gramling & Forsyth, 1987, p. 401).

## Make the Essay Yours

A great essay ultimately brings about change in readers, change in the world. This next essay, by disclosing details that the public at large is unacquainted with, does that. But quotations form the bulk of the argument. There is little of the writer in this piece, little if any original thought; it reads like an article from *Canadian Scientific Journal.* An essay is not a litany of facts; it is an argument, a discussion. It moves toward something.

### Transgender Economics

Transgender people experience various forms of danger, including physical, which occurs to nearly half of surveyed first-world transgender individuals (Lombardi, Wilchins, Priesing, & Malouf, 2002). Another danger is economic, because "for transgender persons of color, [the unemployment] rate increases to four times the national average … over 30 percent of transpersons of color are unemployed" (HuffPost, 2017). Financial income is not the only economic barrier to transgender people; health care is very difficult to attain, as within Alberta, only two doctors work in sex reassignment surgery, and private doctors rarely aid in this (Trans Health Care, 2017). Usually when an individual wishes to transition, two medical procedures present themselves: transgender hormone therapy or previously mentioned sex reassignment surgery. Fortunately for transgender Americans, 77 percent have purchased health insurance to cover transgender related practitioners and 81 percent have seen a doctor in regard to hormone usage; however, they were only able to access a physician if they reduced high-risk behaviour such as smoking (Sanchez, Sanchez,

> & Danoff, 2009). According to one article, individuals who are not covered by their health insurance should anticipate $1,500 per year for hormone treatment, and gender reassignment surgery is a two-year process costing at minimum $30,000 in the United States. Other surgeries such as facial feminization surgery or breast augmentation can bring the minimum total medical cost of transgender living to $172,500, assuming 75 years of hormone treatment (Bradford, 2017). This treatment does not include primary care such as mental health services, reproductive options, or communication therapy (Coleman et al., 2012). Combining transgender unemployment with the lack of healthcare availability may force transgender people to give up their desires so they can continue living outside of poverty; it is certain that any transgendered individual will have economic conflict if they want to fit in with the opposite gender. However, economic sacrifice is almost always met with 100 percent satisfaction if the individual chooses to engage in surgery (Nelson, Whallett, & McGregor, 2009).

Another point you perhaps noticed is this: the topic sentence promises a discussion about the physical dangers of being transgender, but the argument itself is largely about economic danger. If you find your essay getting away on you, especially when you're writing in class under a time constraint, simply change the topic sentence—or the thesis, if the problem is on a larger scale.

## Employ Quotations Don't Explain Them

This writer integrates quotations well; they are seamless, as though they were part of her own sentences. But remember, your goal is not to define or explain quotations; it is to *employ* them to expound on your own arguments. If you find yourself repeating phrases like "this shows" or "this means," you're probably explaining quotations rather than using them to support your own argument.

### Lance Armstrong: It's All About the Bike

Armstrong also states that he grew up in a "dreary one-bedroom apartment" while his mother "worked part-time and finished school" (It's Not About the Bike, p. 18). But Armstrong's mother told him, "Make every obstacle an opportunity" (p. 16), and that's what Armstrong did. In fifth grade he joined the long-distance running team and the local swim club and became a powerful competitor in both sports (p. 22). When he joined the swim club, he was put in with the seven-year-olds because his technique was so poor (p. 22). This shows that Armstrong had a great deal of perseverance, dedication, and determination to succeed. Soon he began to compete in triathlons and won all of his races. "If it was a suffer-fest, I was good at it" (p. 23). This shows that even at a young age, Armstrong wanted to win and would go to any lengths to do so.

## Editorial Eye

Sometimes your writing might include an awkward sequence of ideas, such as that underlined in the sentences that follow:

> In fifth grade he joined the long-distance running team and the local swim club and became a powerful competitor in

> both sports (p. 22). When he joined the swim club, he was put in with the seven-year-olds because his technique was so poor (p. 22). This shows that Armstrong had a great deal of perseverance, dedication, and determination to succeed.

We learn that he became a powerful competitor in running and swimming before we find out he was a weak swimmer when he started out. Try to fit your ideas into a smoother sequence, as follows:

> In fifth grade he joined the long-distance running team and the local swim club. At first, Armstrong swam with the seven-year-olds because his technique was so poor (p. 22). In time, however, he became a powerful competitor in both sports, showing that Armstrong had a great deal of perseverance, dedication, and determination to succeed.

---

## Use Long Quotations Effectively

It's tempting, I recognize, to fill the page with long quotations in order to generate the required 2500 words. But typically, fluffing up an essay will lower your grade and, more importantly, dilute your arguments.

> **Perception, Power, and Social Mobility**
>
> In May 1821, Napoleon was executed. Louis XVIII took the throne, and life in France changed drastically again. Social mobility, believed to be one of Napoleon's great achievements, came to an end, and so did many of his laws and ideas. This is revealed in *The Red and the Black* when Julien, a young peasant boy living in France, has

to deal with the struggles of an average peasant citizen during the early 19th century:

> I am called Julien Sorel, madame; I am extremely nervous at entering a strange house for the first time in my life, and I will need your protection and forgiveness for a lot of things in the first few days. I have never been to school, I was too poor; and I have never spoken to anyone except my cousin the surgeon-major, a member of the Legion of Honour, and M, le Cure Chelan. He will speak up for me to you. My brothers have always beaten me, don't believe them if they speak ill of me to you. Excuse my faults, madame, I shall never mean any harm. (p. 38)

I'm not convinced that a 109-word quotation is needed to establish that Julien struggles as an "average peasant." This quotation could have been summarized in a dozen or so words.

The writer goes on to list several more short and long quotations without inserting any of her own thoughts.

> This class division not only affects people's opportunities and behaviour. It affects their thoughts and perceptions. Julien is obsessed with the upper classes and their money: "She's a beautiful noble being, I'm the son of a worker, she loves me..." (p. 127). But in spite of his admiration for the rich, he despises them: "On his part, he felt nothing but hatred and disgust for the superior society into which he was admitted—at the lower end of the table, it is true, which perhaps throws light on the hatred and the disgust" (p. 43). However, despite his disgust for the upper class, there are many times when he lusts after their money, and wishes he were an

aristocrat. He even pretends to be one of them, thinking he has more power than he actually does:

> At that moment he felt completely aristocratic—he who for so long had been so offended by the patronizing smirk and complacent superiority he thought to lie behind all the politeness he was offered. He could not help feeling the great difference. (p. 153)

Julien clearly has a hard time deciphering the difference between his fantasies and the reality of class division:

> To hear himself called "monsieur" again, in full seriousness, and by so beautifully dressed a lady, was quite beyond all Julien's dreams: in all his youthful castles in Spain he had told himself that a real lady would only deign to speak to him when he was dressed in handsome uniform. (p. 36)

He even refers to the lower classes as though he were not one of them: "See how enthusiasm increases the numbers of these peasants, thought Julien" (p. 113). Yet Julien isn't the only one putting on airs. It seems as though everyone seeks to be in a higher position than the next person:

> Everything there was magnificent and new, and one was told the price of each article of furniture. Julien found something ignoble in all this, smelling misappropriated funds. Everyone, down even to the servants, had an air of putting on confident looks in order to avert contempt. (p. 150)

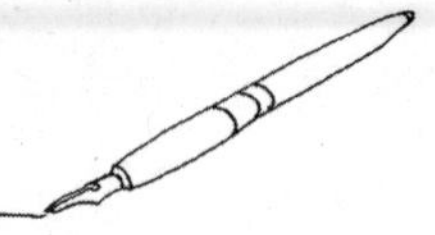

## Editorial Eye

A common problem in writing is using a weak, vague sentence opening such as "This is," or "It is." Make it part of your routine to scour your work for such openings to clarify what "this" or "it" means. In the writing below, what is revealed? The end of social mobility? The end of Napoleon's laws and ideas?

> In May 1821, Napoleon was executed. Louis XVIII took the throne, and life in France changed drastically again. Social mobility, believed to be one of Napoleon's great achievements, came to an end, and so did many of his laws and ideas. This is revealed in *The Red and the Black* when Julien, a young peasant boy living in France, has to deal with the struggles of an average peasant citizen during the early 19th century:

---

## Avoid Plagiarism

Using too many quotations is the most common and egregious error that I see in undergraduate essays. One solution, I suppose, is to avoid citing sources altogether and present a litany of Internet quotations that are impossible to trace, as the next writer does—but it could earn you an F for plagiarism. The following excerpt reads like a Wikipedian avatar. This is perhaps why the writer is experiencing difficulty; he includes no claims or ideas of his own and thus is reluctant to place a citation after every sentence.

> **Peasants and Paupers**
>
> At the end of the medieval period in Europe—specifically, the end of the 1400s and the beginning

> of the 1500s—social life for commoners and peasants was very demanding and difficult; many of them lived unfulfilling and short lives. Social hierarchy was broken up into three estates that was determined by an individual's family, tax bracket, and wealth. Ninety percent of the population fell into the third estate faction and had little to no freedom or power, as the first two estates—the clergy and nobility—had full control and the highest social status in Europe. Most commoners lived in small, cramped countryside villages or towns with their families. Women stayed home and cared for the home and the children, while men worked as merchants, blacksmiths, shoemakers, or weavers, bringing in a small amount of income—after much of it was pilfered by the clergy and nobility for tithes and taxes. The nobility, specifically lords and vassals, controlled basic rural organization and decided where the peasants could own land, and build their homes and family farms. This was an essential component of feudalism, local and regional governmental structures, and political regimes of Europe at this time.

Some students attempt to avoid plagiarism by rearranging a few words in the quotation. For example, perhaps I want to discuss in an essay the following information in the excerpt:

> Women stayed home and cared for the home and the children, while men worked as merchants, blacksmiths, shoemakers, or weavers, bringing in a small amount of income—after much of it was pilfered by the clergy and nobility for tithes and taxes.

I decide to rearrange the sentence so that it reads as follows:

> Women were homemakers while men worked as labourers, bringing in a menial income—much of which was pilfered by clergy and nobility.

Notice that I've significantly changed the sentence—yet the core ideas still are not mine because I am uniformed about medieval Europe—so I have to cite my source. But at what point do ideas become my own? How many books must I read about a topic before I am no longer obliged to cite sources? Indeed, the line between academic integrity and plagiarism can at times be a thin one.

Allow me to illustrate. Suppose you spend most of your winter days in the backcountry—skiing, ice climbing, snowshoeing, and caving—and when you're not in the backcountry, you're reading about it. You could probably write a book about avalanche safety using few if any sources apart from a few official resources to substantiate your data. Yet if *I* were to write such a book, I would need to conduct a significant amount of research—and I would have to cite my sources. So the question remains: how would I write such a book without plagiarizing or relying too heavily on quotations?

It is always appropriate to begin the writing process by prereading—by garnering a swath of general information about the topic that is well known to the majority of scholars in the field. If at this point you decide to write an essay, you are no longer required to cite sources because you have internalized information that is, in essence, common knowledge. But the question is this: why would you want to write about a ubiquitous topic that has already been poked and prodded? The goal of an academic essay, remember, is to *say something*—to engage your reader.

To return to our example about medieval Europe, if I am using my paraphrased sentence above, then I am perhaps exploring something related to exploitation or the division of labour, and I want to use the quotation as an *impetus* for a fresh and perceptive discussion. In short, I want to use the **CSI** approach.

## Apply Theories to New Contexts

I have stressed that an important part of the undergraduate research process is gleaning from the wisdom of others: conducting research, assimilating it, saying something about it, and ideally constructing new ideas around the topic. An effective way of doing this is to apply the theories you are learning to new contexts. The following student applies Emile Durkheim's theories to an American rehabilitation program for inmates, the Wild Horse Program.

### Wild Horses: Rehabilitating Inmates

The Wild Horse Program might sound like a vacation for inmates, but it improves the balance between social control and deviant behaviour. The program demonstrates what Emile Durkheim called an *organic society* when he developed the idea of societies becoming more complex, evolving from mechanical to organic solidarity. In organic societies, although individuals perform different tasks and often have different values and interests, their order and very solidarity depends on their reliance on each other to perform their specified tasks. Organic here is referring to the interdependence of the component parts. Thus, social solidarity is maintained in complex societies through the interdependence of their component parts (e.g., farmers produce the food to feed the factory workers who produce the tractors that allow the farmer to produce the food).

After spending multiple hours conducting research for a paper, it can be difficult to know where your ideas begin and someone else's end. This student does, in fact, give credit to Durkheim for the terminology, but she does not cite her sources.

The next excerpt applies Giorgio Agamben's theories to the homeless population in Calgary.

> **Dominating the Homeless**
>
> Everyday people in Calgary showcase Agamben's state of exception through their dominant behaviour toward people on the streets. Dominance is about exerting authority or influence, so a dominant character signifies a superior and assertive makeup of someone. Allan Mazur, the author of *Biosociology of Dominance and Deference*, describes "the dominance hierarchy to be fairly persistent, unequal ranking in terms of power, influence and valued prerogatives" (2005, p. 7). We, everyday people, possess an unspoken authority in Calgary among the homeless camp—an authority that continues each year. Mazur claims that once dominance has been established, it holds on as the individuals involved recognize their place: "established hierarchies are accepted as normal by force of tradition" (2005, p. 7). Through rooted practice, everyday people display dominance towards marginalized people in verbal and non-verbal expressions. "Everything is truly possible" in the relations of the everyday people to the marginalized (Agamben, 2000, p. 41).

No doubt, Agamben is a difficult philosopher to understand, and this writer has presented some of his more compelling theories.

But like many writers, she relies too heavily on quotations. The first two quotations are intriguing, although she should give examples of what this dominant behavior is. But the last one is ambiguous. How is everything "truly possible" if there is rooted practice in the dominance hierarchy? Is the writer saying that bad things can and do happen to marginalized people? And is the phrase "everything is truly possible" so unique to Agamben's thinking that it is indispensable to the delineation of his theories? Remember that you can use only a limited number of quotations, so choose those that effectively convey the theorist's ideas and serve to advance your claims.

## Think It Through

The following writer is beginning to acclimatize herself to the **CSI** method: she makes a claim, supports it with evidence from secondary sources, and unpacks the quotations with a beautiful image at the end. Notice her use of detail: women bound like their feet; embroidered silk shoes covering rotting skin, broken bones and deformation. Such imagery enriches an academic essay if it is used with discretion. However, there are problems with her use of quotations—see whether you can find them.

### Chinese Foot Binding

Although women gained status and security through marriage, they were sometimes as broken on the inside as their toes were. Many struggled with feelings of worthlessness and meaninglessness. If women showed any emotion and tried to stand up for themselves, it was forbidden. Women were not encouraged to express themselves or to grow as individuals. Their appearance always had to be neat and tidy, even in front of their family and husband; they had to be virtually flawless

(*Women's Virtues and Vices*, p. 18, 19). Everything revolved around *putting others above themselves*: "The stunted growth of Chinese womanhood may be said to owe its origin to the psychological suggestion of society that a virtuous woman should be obedient, quiet, *self-effacing* and ignorant, devoting herself only to the *service of the family*. There is no actual persecution or suppression of feminine activities" (*Chinese Women*, p. 78). Women were expected to *hide their feelings* and *serve the family*—they were as bound as their feet: "Humility means yielding and acting respectful, *putting others first and oneself last*, never mentioning one's own good deeds or denying one's own faults, enduring all insults and bearing with mistreatment, all with due trepidation. Industriousness means going to bed late, getting up early, never shirking work morning or night, never refusing to take on domestic work, and completing everything that needs to be done neatly and carefully. Continuing the sacrifices means serving one's husband-master with appropriate demeanor, keeping oneself clean and pure, never joking or laughing, and preparing pure wine and food to offer the ancestors" (*Women's Virtues and Vices*, p. 18). One must question, however, how women felt underneath the perfection, whether they truly were happy serving everyone but themselves. Most likely, the beauty on the outside covered up stunted growth on the inside, just as their embroidered shoes of silk covered rotting skin, broken bones and deformed feet.

Here, the writer is largely summarizing quotations, as I've pointed out by italicizing similar ideas. She has also missed the intent of the first direct quotation. The quotation stresses that the stunted growth of Chinese womanhood was due to societal expectations rather than persecution or suppression, but the student uses it to support her claim that Chinese women were bound and broken.

Notice also that her quotations are quite long. I mentioned earlier that when you use a long quotation, you should quote only the words that are needed to convey your idea. I would be hesitant to shorten the final quotation because it is powerful and fluid. However, it reiterates the ideas in the paraphrase from *Women's Virtues and Vices* and the first direct quotation (from *Chinese Women*)—and consequently, the argument is almost entirely composed of paraphrases and quotations. Something has to go. I would likely eliminate the paraphrase and first direct quotation and discuss the final long quotation in detail—after consulting a citation guide about how to incorporate long quotations into an essay (hint: they have to be free-standing and indented).

But here's the rub: when you cut quotations, you cut words—and you have to fill the page. The question is, then, what do you *say* in a discussion about your evidence? How do you include your own ideas without leaning too heavily on quotations?

An insightful analysis doesn't point to *what is*—the brokenness, the worthlessness and meaninglessness. Leave that to the quotations. Rather, the I parts of your paper should talk about the *how* or the *why* or the *implications*. The following dialogue, I hope, adds clarity.

**A**: Many Chinese women felt worthless.

**B**: Why?

**A**: Because their feet were bound.

**B**: Why?

**A**: Because society deemed that bound feet were beautiful.

**B**: Women's feet were broken and rotting. How was that beautiful?

**A**: Because they were small and hidden behind silk.

**B**: So the important thing is what's on the outside. Why was smallness and hiddenness deemed beautiful?

**A**: Because their feet were delicate, I suppose. And that made women dependent.

**B**: Why did delicate feet make them dependent?

**A**: Because of a lack of mobility.

**B**: Is there a relationship between mobility and independence?

**A**: I have to think about that. I think so.

**B**: What were some other impacts of foot binding?

**A**: The broken toes caused women to walk in a way that was alluring to men, swaying their hips. The more sexually attractive women were, the better they married.

**B**: Why was it important to marry well?

**A**: Survival! Women lacked status.

**B**: Why?

**A**: Because they had no power.

**B**: Why do some people thrive on the lack of power in others?

You can see, I hope, that this dialogue—this asking *why*—brings us deeper into the issues. If you lack confidence in your ability to delve into a topic, read some of Plato's dialogues—*Ion* or *Republic* or *Laws*—and then try to personalize the topic. You perhaps have little to say about Chinese foot binding, but can you think of people in your immediate surroundings who lack power?

As an undergraduate, I worked in a bank to pay for my education. One of the customer service agents was slow on her feet and slow in speech, and the staff were merciless with her. She never responded to their taunts; she seemed unaffected. And so they taunted her even more. Why? Why did her unresponsiveness attract greater antagonism? Why didn't she fight back? Why couldn't her coworkers tolerate weakness? Or *was* she weak? What *is* weakness? What do these things tell us about human nature? Can I apply some of those observations to foot binding?

## Use Case Studies

The following writer conducted primary research to delineate Giorgio Agamben's theories. She interviewed a middle-aged man who panhandles in in downtown Calgary all day every day and calls himself Day-All Day (pronounced *Dale-Day*). This essay is not a compilation of quotations; it expresses the genuine thoughts of the writer.

### The Homeless Camp

Everyday people force marginalized individuals away from the general public. My friend, Day-All Day, describes the public in Calgary as "everyday people" and "not so everyday people" (personal communication, April 20th, 2018). When I first met Day-All, I sat down on the street beside him to hear his stories. Men walked by, their heads high as they passed, friends walked their dogs, chatted and never looked our way. But there were a few people who slowed to dig for coins in their pockets. There is a distinct separation between the classes of people here—a separation we observe with our eyes. We live as if a high cement wall existed between us, and we are

> unable to see each other, hear each other, or help one another. The Proverbs warn that "...those who close their eyes to poverty will be cursed" (28:27, NLT). Day-All told me this obvious separation "comes from high class and no class" (personal communication, April 20th, 2018). High-class people have jobs where they are seen every day such as teachers, lawyers, pastors, photographers—most of Calgary—and these people create the standard of life. We are the sovereign power, and our habits, transitioned into lifestyles, press marginalized people into their camp: homelessness.

The case study sets up the essay. From that point, the writer incorporates relevant quotations from another primary source, Viktor E. Frankl's book *Man's Search for Meaning*, in an application of Agamben's notion of camps.

> Although everyday people create physical barriers that create marginalization, each person has a choice in the *mental* barrier. We choose our mental perspective in each circumstance; our minds are not the default of events. Viktor E. Frankl, author of *Man's Search for Meaning* (2006), argues that "everything can be taken from a man but one thing: the last of the human freedoms—to choose one's attitude in any given set of circumstances, to choose one's way" (p. 66). Frankl endured gruesome torture in concentration camps; he watched men die beside him and faced endless little problems within ceaseless persecution. Yet he advocates that one can include human integrity in all situations. Through any set of circumstances—in every situation—we get to choose

> our attitude. This concept translates into a theory that psychologist Albert Bandura (1994) defines as self-efficacy: one's belief in one's ability to succeed in specific situations.

The writer then employs Albert Bandura's theories about self-efficacy to discuss homelessness. Below, she uses a long quotation to convey Day-All's thoughts—far more powerful than using a short or indirect quotation in this situation:

> Therefore, within Day-All's high state of self-efficacy, he holds hope for his future. He told me about his dream to talk on the radio, and he knew how it would happen:
>
> > All right—do you hear my voice? Do you think it's a nice voice? I want to take a course at SAIT for broadcasting. I want to be on the radio [he said with a big smile]. I've basically learned how to sing under this tunnel as I've sat out here for six years. Like I said, the word *can't* doesn't exist in my vocabulary. So the driver's licence, I'll accomplish that and I'll accomplish a vehicle. And I'm going to go to SAIT, and I'll learn how to talk on the radio. Does that sound cool to you? (personal communication, April 20, 2018)
>
> Though Day-All currently sits on the streets to collect money, he sees the good and he chooses to see good in his future. Like Frankl and Bandura write and as Day-All lives, in every given set of circumstances, we are able to choose hope.

This writer has effectively delineated Agamben's theories without exhausting the reader with a litany of quotations. But how did she get there? How do you write authentically while satisfying the rigours of an academic assignment?

Ultimately, your professor wants you to *say something*, and to do that, you have to take time to *think*. You have to slow your pace—as though you were reading a Dickens novel. It's a different frame of mind; imagine that you've just relocated from the frenetic pace of a large city to a quiet maritime town. Be quiet, be still, and *think*.

*To write well, you have to take time to think. You have to slow your pace—as though you were reading a Dickens novel.*

If you are faced with a difficult theory, try to reduce it to the lowest common denominator in order to gain insight. For example, when my daughter was in grade ten social studies, she was grappling with theories related to communism and capitalism. We talked at length about the possibility of opening a small jewelry kiosk in her school. How would the experience differ under each form of government? With that frame of reference, she was able to say something intelligible about the ideologies—something real, something all her own, something from the gut.

## Critique a Theory

Another effective strategy is to critique a theorist, as the following writer does in an analysis of Dan Stone's *Genocide as Transgression*. In the first paragraph, he employs several quotations to establish what he is critiquing. He then uses the Rape of Nanking and the Rwandan genocide to delineate his own theories about why genocide occurs.

### Genocide as Festival

As Stone continues with his analysis of the mechanics behind genocide, he describes "ecstatic participation" as a function of "ecstatic communities." He says that within a festival, there is the sense of ecstatic participation that is enjoyed by individual participants. He describes it as a "license to indulge in frenzied transgression of norms and laws" and that it is a "time for personal release just as much as it is a time of social revivification" (Stone, 2004, p. 53). In relating this idea to genocide and war, Stone explains that groups of people need to indulge in mass killing and murdering in order to release a buildup of stress, anger and tension. This is why he says that mass murder is the norm (p. 49), because every person has this need for release at various points in life and for varying reasons.

Neither the Rape of Nanking nor the Rwandan genocide are examples of a country experiencing ecstatic community or participation, as Stone defines them. They are examples of how feelings of rage and hatred can build up over a long period of time because of a lack of power and independence. The Hutus and Japanese did not perform mass murder because they needed to purge their feelings of anger and tension; it wasn't simply a time for "personal release." Nor did they behave as they did because they wanted to "indulge," as Stone puts it, as if they were indulging in the last

> piece of chocolate cake. When ethnic and political frictions are constructed, groups of people do not fight to release their own emotions; they do it for the sake of their country and independence, for things that are more imperative and central. Stone defines the idea of genocide too casually when he uses examples like this as well as when he uses terms such as "indulge" or "personal release."

I would prefer that in the second paragraph the writer use specific evidence to support his claims. For example, he says that "groups of people do not fight to release their own emotions; they do it for the sake of their country and independence, for things that are more imperative and central." What specific examples from Nanking and Rwandan history support this claim?

## Editorial Eye

Be as precise as possible in your word choices to ensure your ideas are clear and sharp. You might not do this in your first draft, but in second and subsequent drafts, look closely at the words you use and think about what they mean. For example, take a close look at a few word choices in the following writing selection.

> Nor did they behave as they did because they wanted to "indulge," as Stone puts it, as if they were indulging in the last piece of chocolate cake. When ethnic and political frictions are constructed, groups of people do not fight to release their own emotions;

The phrase "When ethnic and political frictions are constructed" suggests an activity—we're making frictions. I'm not sure that's what you intend here. Isn't it more about being in the context of ethnic and political frictions? In the face of them? So perhaps revise to something like "In the midst of ethnic and political frictions" or "Chafed with ethnic and political frictions."

> they do it for the sake of their country and independence, for things that are more imperative and central. Stone defines the idea of genocide too casually when he uses examples like this as well as when he uses terms such as "indulge" or "personal release."

Here's one of those vague pronouns. Like which? Which specific example are we talking about? Or are we talking about many examples, such as Nanking and Rwanda? Could this sentence be recast to read "Stone defines the idea of genocide too casually, using terms such as "indulge" or "personal release" in relation to the horrors of XX [whatever examples you mean in this sentence]."

---

Later in the essay, he makes a similar point: that people do not behave in ways that exemplify Stone's theories. He lists several examples of atrocities committed against specific people groups but doesn't specify why these examples counter Stone's arguments. It is not enough to make a claim; you must prove it with specific and compelling examples and an explanation about why these examples support your claim (**I**).

> Stone states that rather than "exceptional psychopaths" committing violent crimes in society, it is, in a time of psychic stress, "ordinary people [who] are able to take part in collective acts of extreme violence of which they would otherwise never have suspected themselves capable" (p. 57). For Stone, war and genocide are about ordinary people coming together and taking part collectively in a bonding event in society, much like a festival. But instead of celebrating, these ordinary people are purifying their society through murder. Here, mass murder is normal in certain contexts, and arises every few years because "all societies require periods of collective effervescence in order to break free from the monotony

> of everyday life" (p. 53). But in reality, when individuals are bored by dullness and uniformity, they do not resort to genocide in an effort to animate their lives, as the consequences, seen in the Rwandan, Cambodian, and Chinese genocides, are unimaginably vast. People do not perform such actions, knowing these consequences, in order to simply break out of the norm. There are countless motivations that dig much deeper.

In this excerpt, Stone compares genocide with the elements of a festival, using historic genocides to support his claim. But do these examples of genocide in fact exhibit elements of festival, or is Stone taking leaps of logic? Does Stone employ I's in his approach, or does he merely juxtapose claims and support without explaining their connection?

The student is using the **CSI** method to analyze Stone's work and spot flaws in his argument. Do the examples of genocide that Stone uses exhibit elements of festival, or is he taking leaps of logic? By understanding the **CSI** method, you will also be able to examine the logic in others' arguments and respond to their theories with confidence and insight.

**task** Review the examples above that best represent your challenges in using quotations. Then edit your "Marrakech" essay, focussing on the **CSI** approach.

13

# Transitioning Between Arguments

We touched on transitions in Take Three, and I now want to discuss them in greater detail. Strong transitions are the mark of a refined writer; if your essay flows naturally and logically from one idea to the next, it is more powerful, more enjoyable to read.

## Artificial Transitions

I want to emphasize that there is nothing inherently wrong with artificial transitions if they are not overused or used to force connections where none exist. The following excerpt uses the artificial transition *similarly*. Do you think it works?

> This event caused the brother to take matters into his own hands. He wanted to buy something from the store, but he wasn't allowed to. This causes him to make a decision that is on the downswing of morality. He does something unexpected: "He smiled faintly, reached into his coat pocket. 'Here. Have one of these.' . . . 'You *stole* these?' 'Yeah. It's easy.'" Would the brother have stolen if the clerk had treated him like a White boy? No, he has a

> vendetta. This is evident from the contrast of tears and smiles when he succeeded in his theft (p. 52). The brother found joy in stealing from an adversary who brought him pain. When the brother's freedom of choice was taken, his morality shifted downward to commit a crime he otherwise wouldn't have committed.
>
> Similarly, Frankl's book is set in the concentration camps of the Holocaust. Time after time, freedom of choice was stolen from the prisoners. Their very existence lay in the hands of one person's opinion. The very first decision made for them was right or left, life or death: "It was the first selection, the first verdict made on our existence or non-existence" (Frankl, 2006, p. 12). The prisoners were told what to do, where to go—they had no choice. Ultimately, the very choice of continuing to live was the only choice they had left.

Notice that the word *similarly* is comparing a boy's moral choice with a concentration camp. This is not a valid comparison. The topic sentence in the second argument should instead say something like this:

> Similarly, in Frankl's book, freedom of choice is stolen from prisoners in the concentration camps of the Holocaust.

In this way, we are comparing the freedom of choice of two groups of people. It is an artificial transition, but it works well because the controlling idea of free choice is threaded through both paragraphs.

However, your arguments should be logical and believable. The writer states that a boy who steals does not have a choice because of the way he is treated by a clerk. Such a contention is counter-intuitive—and the antithesis of Frankl's assertion that humans always have the freedom to choose their attitude, and thus their way, in a given set of circumstances.

## Natural Transitions

Natural transitions thread the thesis through arguments and paragraphs without the aid of artificial transitions such as *in addition*, *by contrast*, *firstly*, *finally*, and so on. Below are several examples of how you can transition between ideas without constructing a forced, starched essay.

## Using Words and Ideas

The following essay, concerned with the weight of social stigmas, transitions between paragraphs by describing first the physical adjustments of acquiring prosthetics—then the social ones.

> **End paragraph 2**: He had a wheelchair and prosthetic legs to accommodate him, but the simplest tasks became a challenge for him: going up and down stairs, picking up small items from the floor.
>
> **Begin paragraph 3**: The most significant adjustments, however, came from dealing with the perceptions of those around him.

The next essay applies Giorgio Agamben's theories about camps to elements of Canadian society. The writer must transition between Canadian prisons and Canadian refugees—a difficult task indeed, because the topics at first appear to be unrelated.

> **End paragraph 18**: It is fair to say that we do see parts of Agamben's camps in Canada's detainment centres, based on the personal accounts of individuals who have spent time in them and related them to a prison.

> **Begin paragraph 19**: When refugees enter the country, they, like prisoners, are immediately separated from the rest of society and forced into unknown terrain.

According to this writer, the connection between prison life and seeking refuge is perhaps more immediate than we would care to admit.

In the following essay, the writer uses the term *mutual intelligibility* to transition naturally between paragraphs.

> **End paragraph 4**: This information provided through Heeringa et al.'s research is virtually a map that indicates the ease of mutual intelligibility between the two languages.
> **Begin paragraph 5**: Mutual intelligibility can be examined from both the written and the spoken aspects of a language.

## Using Chronology

If your essay is chronological, transitioning is quite simple—but there is a danger of simply recounting facts and not owning the essay. The following writer moves fluidly from one paragraph to the next, examining the phenomenon and ultimate collapse of Lance Armstrong's rhetoric. Sometimes specific words or phrases are repeated between paragraphs, and sometimes words like "yet," "although" and "however" are used to indicate turning points in the progression of the story.

> **End paragraph 4**: Here, Armstrong develops a rhetoric that convinces us that he is an ordinary person. And ordinary people do not do drugs.
> **Begin paragraph 5**: Yet while writing his autobiography, Armstrong was involved in the "biggest fraud in the history of sport" (CNN).
> **End paragraph 5**: Herrick states that "a rhetor must consider what an audience accepts as true, probable, or desirable,"

and that the audience "has the major role in determining the quality of the argument ... of orators" (p. 10). Armstrong knew that the audience decides what is true and what isn't, not the rhetor, and he worked hard to persuade the public that he was innocent.

**Begin paragraph 6**: While the rhetoric of the individual—Lance Armstrong—was powerful, it was upheld and strengthened by the rhetoric of the collective. Despite the evidence that cycling and Armstrong were involved in doping, cycling fans wanted a hero.

**End paragraph 6**: Although the public suspected that Armstrong was doing drugs, they chose to ignore it because in their eyes he was a hero.

**Begin paragraph 7**: In 2012, however, things changed. Armstrong was removed as the Chairman of Livestrong, and in 2012 the United Cycling Institution (UCI) stripped Armstrong of his seven titles. All along, even though the public knew he was guilty, they supported him, but in 2012, a shift in rhetoric occurred.

**End paragraph 7**: When the rhetoric moved from the scientific community of the UCI and the World Anti-doping Association (WADA) to Armstrong's peers, the public was finally convinced.

**Begin paragraph 8**: Once the collective was convinced of Armstrong's guilt, they were determined to remove him from his pedestal.

Notice that the thesis—that Armstrong's rhetoric gained power only until his peers publicly denounced him—is threaded through each argument and gains momentum as the essay progresses, like jam in a Viva Puff. The essay does not merely chronicle the events of a doping scandal; it moves inexorably toward answering the question of why rhetoric can be so powerful that it subsumes people's beliefs.

In the next essay, the student was asked to write about the Napoleonic era, and sensing that the topic was too broad, she narrowed it to social mobility under Napoleon.

> **Begin paragraph 2**: Before Napoleon ruled France, the monarchy held the power, made the decisions and created the laws, many of which were outdated and traditional.
>
> **End paragraph 2**: The majority of society under the monarchy was frustrated and ready for new leadership and new ideas; they were ready for the Napoleonic era.
>
> **Begin paragraph 3**: In 1804, the Napoleonic Code was established.
>
> **End paragraph 3**: All of this resulted in "a shifting of power from the former privileged classes to a wider elite of persons who drew income from the soil."
>
> **Begin paragraph 4**: Napoleon felt that the lower classes were important and needed in society because, being the majority, they formed most of the work force and held the economy together.
>
> **End paragraph 4**: The upper classes didn't share Napoleon's views: they wanted more power than the lower classes had, and certainly didn't want to be on the same social and economic level as the rest of society.
>
> **Begin paragraph 5**: Napoleon, however, held the keys: the Napoleonic Code.
>
> **End paragraph 5**: But how long could the external pressure of law control the internal forces of man?
>
> **Begin paragraph 6**: In May 1821, Napoleon died in exile.

In paragraph 2, the writer describes the lack of social mobility under the monarch: people talked about freedom and honour and order, but these ideals were not a reality for most of the population, particularly for the peasants. This discussion sets the stage for paragraph 3, which outlines the Napoleonic Code and the social mobility that it created. Paragraph 4 outlines the class tensions that ensued, and paragraphs 5 and 6 describe the ultimate failure of Napoleon's strategies. This essay is not a mere recounting of events; each argument builds on the previous one to construct an argument about social mobility in the Napoleonic era. It moves through the historical events chronologically, but it doesn't transition in a clunky or obvious way.

## Expanding on Ideas

The following writer transitions effectively from one paragraph to the next by expanding on ideas in each successive paragraph. In this way, no idea, no sentence, can be relocated without damaging the whole.

> **End paragraph 11**: But who decides what these standards are? There are no laws that decide where and how much an individual can and cannot tattoo.
>
> **Begin paragraph 12**: Foucault (1977) says that "the judges of normality are present everywhere. We are in the society of the teacher-judge, the doctor-judge, the educator-judge, the social worker-judge" (p. 92). These judges are the undeclared leaders and people we look up to: our managers and coworkers, our parents and family members, our professors and peers.
>
> **End paragraph 12**: Society as a whole, then, still has standards for the tattooed population, and someone with "too many tattoos" or tattoos that are "offensive" or "unpleasant" is scrutinized and judged.
>
> **Begin paragraph 13**: However, the tattoo culture serves to test and critique the prevailing assumptions by entering into what postmodern thinkers call a critical encounter, an *Auseinandersetzung*, a coming together and posing questions, not answering them.

This writer pairs tattoo culture with societal surveillance and expands on his ideas by discussing notions about power—where it comes from, how it is enforced, how it can be monitored. The essay is not a litany of abstracted ideals about power; rather, it narrows the focus to the tattoo phenomenon and in doing so, constructs a compelling analysis indeed.

## Refining an Argument

Another way of transitioning is to delineate an argument in one paragraph and refine it in the next. In the example below, the first paragraph sets forth the idea that athletes' bodies are monitored and judged, and the second narrows the topic to specific sports. Later, the essay will take a philosophical turn and discuss *why* our society—and those in power—prefer some body types over others.

> **End paragraph 11**: Disciplining the body is one of the most important aspects of being an athlete, and whether that means gaining muscle or shedding weight, athletes feel the pressure from inside and outside sources to reach their peak performance levels. Their bodies are diligently watched and monitored by judges, coaches, teammates, fans, and peers; they are examined and policed from head to toe.
>
> **Begin paragraph 12**: Yet according to the American College of Sport Medicine (ACSM), in Michael Brunet's article "Female Athlete Triad," close monitoring of the body appears to be more common in certain types of sports. In sports where performance is subjectively scored such as dance, figuring skating, and gymnastics, female bodies reflect society's concept of a thin, graceful swan in order to look elegant and appealing in the eyes of the audience.

## Presenting a Contrast

The following excerpts discuss the reasons for foot binding in paragraphs 6 and 7 and the negative consequences in paragraph 8.

> **End paragraph 6**: Bound feet were also considered intensely erotic: women had to hobble and sway their hips to walk, and men found this quite alluring. It was also believed that this type of walking strengthened vaginal muscles, improving sexual intercourse.
>
> **End paragraph 7**: Anything that is desirable and sought-after gains status, and status increases social positioning. In order to gain a higher social position, Chinese women needed to attract a man and marry well. It was the only way they could survive.
>
> **Begin paragraph 8**: Although women gained status and security through marriage, they were sometimes as broken on the inside as their toes were.

The underlined sentence above links to arguments in paragraphs 6 and 7, while the word "although" makes it clear that we're starting a turn in the argument.

task

Edit your "Marrakech" essay for transitions. Does it flow well from sentence to sentence, paragraph to paragraph, argument to argument?

# 14

# Refining Introductions and Conclusions

We've talked at length about how to build the body of an essay by constructing arguments and linking them together. Now, somehow, you have to write an introduction and conclusion. A skilled essayist understands that the introduction and conclusion are more than bookends—they show the way: the introduction shows the way *through* the essay, and the conclusion shows the way *after* the essay.

### *Example 1*

> Rebellions are born out of a loss of freedom. Freedom to live, freedom to choose, freedom of your own morality. Often, people are placed outside of the inner circle of society, cast away into a state of exclusion, unwanted. When a man is told he cannot have food, he is then forced to go outside of his moral limits to acquire it. However, once you commit one sin, it is easier to commit another. Thus, the moral standing of man can be taken

> away in the single action of taking away their freedom of choice. In the texts *Blackbird Calling* by Laura Swart and *Man's Search for Meaning* by Viktor E. Frankl, we are shown that when the basic freedom of choice is taken away, the loss of morality is close behind.

This introduction provides a few interesting opening sentences and clearly states the thesis, but it lacks cohesion. What's the connection between the second and third sentences? How does the fourth sentence fit in? This is why our Cut and Paste rule is so important: each sentence, each paragraph, each argument, should lead seamlessly to the one following it. The introduction has also shifted from third- to second-person point of view. The second-person point of view (*you*) is acceptable in tweets and blogs and emails, but not in academic essays.

The conclusion of this essay, unfortunately, merely summarizes the main points, and the quotation at the end seems to contradict the premise of the essay, that free choice doesn't always exist. The final quotation is also detached from the previous sentences and somehow needs to be connected to them.

> When man is left with no choice, the only thing he is left to do is break the constraints of his own mind. This is the cruelest thing anyone can do to a person. In both texts we see a common issue: the freedom of choice was taken away, and immoral thoughts gave birth to actions. The brother in *Blackbird Calling* was forced to leave a store, changing his moral attitude and stealing from that store. In the same way, when the prisoners in the concentration camps were stripped of any and every choice, they were forced to make the immoral decision about whether to survive or give up. When freedom of

> choice is taken away, no matter how large or small, it will bring forth frustration. Frustration brings forth anger, and anger is the father of immorality. "If you do what is right, will you not be accepted? But if you do not do what is right, sin is crouching at your door; it desires to have you, but you must rule over it" (Genesis 4:7, *New International Version*).

### *Example 2*

The next introduction reveals the paper's direction—that the writer will examine stigmatization through a case study—but it doesn't explicitly state the thesis. I find the introduction engaging, however, and as long as the essay moves toward a central claim, I don't mind the omission of a formal thesis statement.

> Normality is something that individuals find security and comfort in; it regulates society and keeps everything safe and familiar. When it is disrupted by people who do not fall within the mean of "normal," society is quick to judge, create labels, and find ways to create a new normal. The stigmatization of individuals with mental or physical differences is an example of this. A stigma is defined as "a discrediting attribute or mark of disgrace that leads others to see us as untrustworthy, incompetent, or tainted. The common bases of stigma are physical deformities, character flaws, and membership in tainted groups" (Sandstrom, Martin & Fine, 2010, p. 197). This definition raises a few questions. Why is a person with a physical deformity or abnormality considered by society as "untrustworthy or incompetent"? Why are so many

> people uncomfortable with differences, with anything out of the norm? Whether it is a facial deformity, a limp, or a missing limb, people stare, behave awkwardly, and treat the person differently. This paper will examine these phenomena within the context of a case study: Michael Scott (not his real name) in 1998 was transformed almost overnight from a healthy, active man to what many considered to be an invalid.

The conclusion comes closer to a thesis—that individuals with disabilities actually shape humanity. The ending is appropriate and satisfying.

> We need to acknowledge that the individuals in society who are different from the norm are the ones who shape humanity, giving it character and individuality, just as Scott has done. It is appropriate, therefore, that the final words of this paper be given to Carly (not her real name), who has cerebral palsy and was a speaker at the Nothing is Wasted conference this year: "I used to depend on others to do everything for me, and I couldn't learn what I could do for myself. When I learned what I could do, I went to Mexico to speak at a CP conference. I gave hope to many people" (2014).

### *Example 3*

In the following introduction, our Cut and Paste rule is exemplified; each sentence leads naturally to the next. The first sentence, however, is hollowed out: it need not be stated—indeed, it *should* not be stated. It bears no resemblance to the colourful candies on the Viva Puff and gives no room for the reader to offer a counter-signature. The thesis statement is also a sweeping generalization that says nothing of import, nothing debatable.

> Europe has undergone substantial changes throughout history, particularly in the last several hundred years. Shifts in societal structures, economics, politics, gender roles, social status, and religion have in some cases caused significant problems—and in others, have sparked new ideas that are still valued today. The transition from medieval Europe to early modern Europe—from the beginning of the 16th century to the end of the 18th century—saw progressive changes that laid the stepping-stones for Europe to centralize and expand its power, ideology, and influence. Using the texts *The Return of Martin Guerre, The Praise of Folly,* and *A Short Account of the Destruction of the Indies,* this paper will outline the innovations Europe made in social, religious, political, and philosophical realms.

The conclusion to this essay is slightly better than the introduction.

> Throughout the 16th, 17th, and 18th centuries, we are able to see a gradual shift in societal structures, religion, politics, and philosophical beliefs that allowed society to build ideas and progress in a new and enlightened way. Each significant event had an effect on the events that followed it, and the advancement that was made allowed society to adapt and evolve throughout the era. The texts *The Return of Martin Guerre, The Praise of Folly,* and *A Short Account of the Destruction of the Indies* only give us a slight idea of how history played out in Europe during this

> progressive period in time. The transformations from the Medieval Era into the Early Modern Era and beyond it are still made visible in society today. Whether it was religious aspects from the Protestant Reformation, or ideologies discovered during the Enlightenment, much of society, and how it circulates, would not be the way it currently is without the changes made in these areas during the Early Modern Era in Europe.

It seems likely that the student was asked to summarize three centuries of European history in 2500 words. When you are given a wide-ranging question such as this, it is best to narrow your topic—with the professor's permission—and discuss a single theme that threads its way through events.

### *Example 4*

The following introduction and conclusion do have a thesis, and the writer is attempting to say something of import; she spent a great deal of time thinking about why the public closed its eyes to the doping scandal, which was at the forefront of the news when she wrote this essay. But I think she can go deeper.

> Cycling has long been celebrated as a sport requiring strength, endurance, and oftentimes fearlessness. But for many years, and especially in the past few years, controversy has tainted the sport because of cheating in international races. This past year, Lance Armstrong, one of the world's most famous cyclists and a hero for conquering cancer, was stripped of his medals and accused by his teammates of using performance-enhancing drugs for his entire cycling career. What accounts for the change in rhetoric, for Armstrong's fall

> from grace? People had long suspected and accused Armstrong, of course, but not until 2012, when he was accused by his peers, did the rhetoric of cycling and of Armstrong move from support and admiration to disgust and disappointment. The rhetoric of the individual, then, can be so powerful that it causes its audience to ignore the truth, to ignore what is right.
>
> [...]
>
> The doping crises in cycling is still working itself out. It remains to be seen whether or not Armstrong will be redeemed; he has lost his titles, sponsorships and much of his prize money. Further legal action and jail time are pending. Armstrong says that he is moving on, that he doesn't want to be distracted from his fight against cancer. He still maintains his innocence. If he confessed to doping, he says, "I would lose the faith of all these cancer survivors. It is not about money for me, it is about the faith that people have put in me over the years. All of that would be erased" (CNN). And still, because Armstrong is such a strong rhetor, we agree with Jay Leno: we still want to believe him.

We all know that rhetoric is powerful, that it can inhibit people's judgement—we need not look further than some of our elected officials to discern that. Thus, the thesis is to some extent self-evident. How, then, could the writer have improved it? Perhaps a few more *why* questions, as I demonstrated on pages 103–104, would be helpful. *Why* do we want to believe Armstrong when we know he is lying? *Why* is rhetoric able to subsume truth?

### *Example 5*

This introduction clearly outlines Giorgio Agamben's theories and indicates what direction the paper will take. I would prefer, however, that the thesis statement be more specific about how the state of exception, as in the case of Hutterites, can strengthen and fulfill people.

> Camping is done outside—to get away from the normalities of life. One cannot camp inside their home, or in the city around their customary services; it has to be done outside the norms of society. In the same way, the state of exception exists in camps. This is how Giorgio Agamben describes the camp in *Means Without End: Notes on Politics*; it is a place where the normal laws of society are suspended, people exist in perpetual oblivion, and the totalitarian state takes control. It is a place of depravity, lifelessness, and destruction of the human soul. However, the camp is not always a degrading place; it can be used to benefit a culture. The state of exception has been abused by many totalitarian states, but it has also been used as the basis of certain cultures. Is the state of exception, then, always a bad thing? Examining the life of Hutterites is a prime example of a camp being acted out in daily life, contrary to the thoughts of Agamben's depiction of the state of exception.

### *Example 6*

I'd like to end this section with two conclusions that, I think you will agree, are powerful and engaging.

The first student, asked to write about Abraham Lincoln, sums up Lincoln's life in a conclusion that is artful and engaging. She ends the essay by opening up a new world through Hans-Georg Gadamer.

> Abraham Lincoln is remembered as a towering figure that helped shaped the American nation. He is honoured at Mount Rushmore, at the Lincoln Memorial, and in every American history course. In the days, months, and years after he was assassinated, American sentiment toward him shifted from distaste to remorse to praise and admiration. Now, with such a large distance from the events of his presidency, we remember what he did for the country but not how he did it. We aren't able to relive or fully comprehend what life was like for the Americans living under Lincoln's presidency; we have forgotten the accusations circulating America regarding his being uneducated, untrustworthy, unreliable, incompetent, and underprepared. We have forgotten the suspicions about hidden and underlying motives. However, if we follow Hans-Georg Gadamer's suggestion and look at both the past and the present, we will have a fuller understanding of historical events and the intimate details intertwined within it.

The second student has a strong sense of the art of essay writing.

> What is made abundantly clear in this work is that even the most absurd of abuses, the most putrid of environments, and the most demeaning societal structures can be justified when the inhabitants crushed by these things are no longer seen as human. A fly may be swatted without a second thought to its value and in

equal measure, an entire people can be trodden upon without any significant moral qualm. Using imagery, analogy, and the elucidation of personal perspective, George Orwell conveys with brutal clarity the fact that beneath the facade of empirical glory lies the twisted absurdity of human life reduced to the movement of flies swarming over a restaurant table.

task

**Edit the introduction and conclusion of your "Marrakech" essay using the above examples as a guide.**

# *TAKE FIVE*

In this section, we'll examine six complete essays and determine whether or not they adhere to the principles outlined in this book. Please read the essays and the discussion with Abigail Red (one of my students) that follows each. You will glean a great deal from Abigail's keen eye, and you will learn along with us.

15

# Sample Essays

## Sample Essay 1

### Pain and Identity

*Blackbird Calling* and *Man's Search for Meaning* are two stories that describe racial segregation. They tell of people groups being isolated and targeted because of their race. Both books explain how these cultural groups were forcefully separated from their society and confined in controlled spatial arrangements. Residential schools and concentration camps may have temporally stripped the people of their cultures; however, a person's identity can never be permanently taken from them.

The First Nations and Jewish people were humiliated as their culture was stripped from them. Upon arrival at the residential schools and the concentration camps, a degrading and demoralizing process took place: the

First Nations children's hair was taken from them—their long braids, an identifier of their culture—were cut off (Swart, 2016, p. 77). Likewise, the Jewish people's hair was shaved: "not only their heads were shorn, but not a hair was left on their entire bodies" (Frankl, 2006, p. 15). They were removed from their culture geographically and in regards to their personal appearance. They had no visible reminders of their culture—all they had were their memories. Even their language was insignificant, because the language being spoken around them was not their own.

At the onset of the First Nations and Jewish people's experience, mass confusion and shock took over. First, the people were taken to an unknown destination. If that's not anxiety-provoking enough, the people around them didn't speak their language, so they had no idea of what was going on. Then there were the thoughts and unknowns of whether your family was dead or not, where were they, and why you were being separated from them. Next came the abuse and suffering coming from the ones in charge.

The character Ni'is in *Blackbird Calling* tells the narrator about the abuse that took place in the residential schools (Swart, 2016, p. 43, 87). Ni'is tells a personal story of his father's experience at the residential schools: "They broke all his fingers. Every time he spoke his language, they broke one of his fingers with a mallet" (p. 87). Equally, the author of *Man's Search for Meaning* explains throughout the entirety of his book the atrocities and the suffering that took place within the camps.

All this abuse and separation from their culture brought on anger and oppression. After being set free from the residential schools and the concentrations camps the people "could not escape the influences of the brutality which had surrounded them in camp life" (Frankl, 2006, p. 90). However, they had a choice. They could choose to remain in the anger and bitterness—wallowing in self-pity—or they could take up their cross, like Viktor Frankl, Ni'is, Bonnie, and Gloria did. Ni'is's parents worked on themselves to heal. It took faith and trust to continue on that path of healing. Ni'is had hope, and he hopes his people "don't get stuck in anger. Because it's over. It's over" (Swart, 2016, p. 43). Ni'is and Gloria don't live as if they have no identity; they still cling to their First Nations teachings. They are artistic and hopeful people who love to teach and befriend the people they come across in life. Viktor Frankl allowed his experience to develop his theory on suffering and further his logotherapy. He didn't live a life of fear and bitterness afterwards, as he explains his experience of the concentration camps: "The crowning experience of all, for the homecoming man, is the wonderful feeling that, after all he has suffered, there is nothing he need fear anymore—except his God" (Frankl, 2006, p. 93).

These characters in the books were affected in major ways by the experiences of the residential school and the concentration camps, but they didn't let it define them. They found beauty in it. "It just looks like complete chaos. But if you stand back and look at it, it's absolutely beautiful. The chaos is part of it. The chaos is beautiful" (Swart, 2016, p. 41).

## Discussion

**L**: Abigail, what did you think of the introduction to this essay?

**A**: I think it introduces the concept really well. It makes the connection between the two groups and defines the outside concepts that will be part of the essay, although it doesn't go very much into the books themselves.

**L**: My perspective is that this introduction gets the job done. As you said, it introduces the texts and the main topic, and it does have a thesis. I'm not sure if I agree that a person's identity "can never be taken from them," and even if that is in fact true, it would be difficult to prove within the confines of these books.

**A**: Yes, most definitely. In fact, this essay ignores opposing ideas. In *Blackbird Calling*, some of the characters, such as Jimmy and Ni'is's father, never recovered their identity. The essay ignored that. But at the same time, thesis statements are supposed to be debatable.

**L**: You bring up a good point. Yes, the thesis should be debatable, but if in the text there's a strong argument against your thesis, you have to address it. As you say, you can't just ignore it. This doesn't mean that there are never details in the text that contradict your thesis; it simply means that you have to account for them.

According to this thesis, the essay will prove that residential schools and concentration camps temporarily strip people of their cultures, but that the victims never permanently lose their identities. The thesis has two parts, so when I'm grading the essay, I'll be looking to see if both parts have been developed. Does the essay do that?

**A**: I think the first part of the thesis is developed relatively well. The essay shows how people are stripped of their cultures and their identities. It tells what was done to people and connects that to stripping away their culture.

**L**: Yes, there is strong evidence of culture being stripped, such as when people's hair was cut when they were taken in to the camps and schools. I think this writer could have talked more about the cultural significance of hair. For example, some First Nations men only cut their hair when grieving the loss of a loved one.

**A**: I thought the first part of the thesis was better supported than the second.

**L**: How do you think the writer could rewrite the second half of the thesis?

**A**: I was thinking more about how the person could prove this part of the thesis—the part that says identity can never be taken away. I felt the writer used a lot of vague words rather than specific examples from the book. He said Ni'is and Gloria are artistic and hopeful people who love to teach and befriend others, but he didn't give examples; he just kind of said it. So maybe he should have given examples of how these individuals regained their identity or culture, rather than just saying that they did.

**L**: The writer does say that Ni'is's parents worked on themselves to heal and that they didn't abandon their traditional cultural teachings. But certainly, more discussion is needed. I think the greatest weakness I see in student essays is that there is one quotation after another with little discussion.

**A**: That makes sense. But I think the second last sentence of the paragraph 2 was a good example of an **I**: *They had no visible reminders of their culture—all they had were their memories.* I think memories are important. We see our culture around us every day, so it would be very difficult for a person *not* to connect that with the loss of something very important.

**L:** The next two paragraphs for me are quite problematic. Did you feel the same way?

**A:** They more just describe what happened rather than really say much about it.

**L:** Yes, those were my thoughts. The third paragraph of the essay is a bleeding paragraph.

**A:** Yes, the concept of language is spread over multiple paragraphs.

**L:** The idea of being removed to an unknown destination is very similar to the previous paragraph. And the paragraph after that is super short. It doesn't really have a purpose; I'm not too sure what it's doing in the essay, apart from talking about the horrible things that happened.

**A:** Yes, it really just says, *this is bad*, rather than giving examples of *why* it was bad. The first paragraph about cutting hair says, this is what happened, this is why it was bad, and this is why it supports my thesis.

**L:** The paragraphs are trying to establish that abuse and atrocities and suffering happened, but that's not really what the essay is about; it's about being stripped of culture. What did you think about the next paragraph?

**A:** I found that it kind of changed concepts halfway through.

**L:** Where does it do that?

**A:** In my mind, when I'm reading an essay, I like structure. So when I read a topic sentence like, *All this abuse and separation from their culture brought on anger and oppression,* that's what I'm expecting the paragraph to be about. Halfway through, it's about healing, and to me, that would have made more sense as a separate paragraph. Maybe the part about all the anger and resentment should have been merged with the previous paragraph, and then there should have been a paragraph break. I think it could have improved the flow.

**L**: That's a really good point, Abigail. Is there anything else you'd like to say about this essay?

**A**: One thing I noticed is that the essay doesn't really have a conclusion; the majority of the final paragraph is a quote. And I didn't know what to think of that.

**L**: You're right. The conclusion is quite short. And even if you look at it proportionately, it's imbalanced. What did you think of the content of the conclusion?

**A**: The first sentence is quite vague; what does it mean to be affected in "major ways"? I think the conclusion restates the thesis well; it includes everything the essay is talking about, even though it's so short. But it pretty much just restates the thesis.

**L**: Yes. In class, we talked about the Viva Puff symbol and the importance of bringing a "new world" into the conclusion that is relevant to the thesis. This essay leaves us with an isolated quotation that is unrelated to the essay; the quotation is about Ni'is's experiences on the reserve, not about restoring identity. So an additional few sentences, I think, could describe the connection between the ostensible chaos of the reserve and the chaos of trauma, giving the reader something compelling to ponder.

## Sample Essay 2

### Crime, Deviance, and Control

Michel Foucault said, "There is no glory in punishing"—and few people in North America today would dispute that prisoners need rehabilitation, not just punishment. Typically, rehabilitation is something that helps people gain more independence after sickness, injury, surgery, or in this case, leaving prison. We don't want people coming out of prison more violent than they were when they entered; we want them restored to a better condition: better for themselves, and better for society. In Canada, fears about re-entry of prisoners into society are causing concerns and disputes, which in turn play on the balancing act between social control and deviance—something that societies have tried to maintain for hundreds of years. In this research essay, I want to explore the values behind two of the leading rehabilitation programs in America—the Prisoner Entrepreneurship Program (PEP) and the Wild Horse Program—and try to determine what the best way to rehabilitate is while maintaining social control and order. While the skills offered in the PEP program are needed by prisoners in society, the Wild Horse Program heals the soul; it digs deeper, and for this reason, I believe that it is the better way to rehabilitate.

Throughout history, authoritative figures have dealt with crime and deviant behaviour using methods varying from torture and execution, to brain biopsies, to diagnoses of mental diseases. No matter what era, what belief or stance people took on crime and deviance, the actions society took to prevent crime were a main priority in gaining social control and conformity. An example of this is the oldest known perspective of deviance, the demonic perspective. It existed in the 14th and 15th centuries and handled criminals and deviant behaviour in the most graphic and violent way: "It suggests that we look for the cause and cure of deviant behavior in the realm of the supernatural. Humans [were] pictured as constantly torn between the supernatural forces of good and evil. When we succumb to the influence of evil forces we are drawn in to deviant behavior" (p. 22). In this view, deviance was caused by an individual being taken over by a devil or a spirit, and torture and execution were the main forms of punishment. Authorities wanted to test the body's limit to see how they could get the spirit out of the individual's body.

Another example of a viewpoint about what crime and deviance are and why they exist was the pathological perspective, which rose to prominence in the late 19th century. Many theorists believed that deviance was a form of mental illness or sickness, and that when an individual committed a crime it was because they were either born with a disease or had developed it over their lifetime. As Stephen Pfohl states: "deviance was the product of a disease which infected the body or mind. Its control demanded a medical-like cure rather than either penance or punishment" (p. 104). Many times, individuals would even undergo brain surgery so that doctors could look at their brains and try to determine what was different between a deviant's brain and a non-deviant's brain.

Many theorists also came to the conclusion that criminals had a specific appearance to them, such as thin lips, a hunched back, a long nose, small eyes, etc. When even the smallest crime was committed, especially by people who fell under these physical appearance categories, they were immediately taken in for examination and given a diagnosis.

All of these perspectives take much of the responsibility off the criminal and blame their actions on different things that were believed to cause crime and deviance. In spite of this, Foucault (1977) suggests that punishment is similar to an act of war:

> It was the effect, in the rites of punishment, of a certain mechanism of power: of a power that not only did not hesitate to exert itself directly on bodies, but was exalted and strengthened by its visible manifestations; of a power that asserted itself as an armed power whose functions of maintaining order were not entirely unconnected with the functions of war; of a power that presented rules and obligations as personal bonds, a breach of which constituted an offence and called for vengeance; of a power for which disobedience was an act of hostility, the first sign of rebellion, which is not in principle different from civil war; of a power that had to demonstrate not why it enforced its laws, but who were its enemies, and what unleashing of force threatened them; of a power which, in the absence of continual supervision, sought a renewal of its effect in the spectacle of its individual manifestations; of a power that was recharged in the ritual display of its reality as "super-power." (p. 54)

In today's society, approaches to social control and dealing with deviance are considered to be much more civilized and cultured than, for example, the demonic perspective. When an individual commits a felony, that individual is sent to prison for a certain amount of time, depending on the severity of the crime. Yet Foucault asserts that "a punishment like forced labor or even imprisonment—mere loss of liberty—has never functioned without a certain additional element of punishment that certainly concerns the body itself: rationing of food, sexual deprivation, corporal punishment, solitary confinement … There remains, therefore, a trace of 'torture' in the modern mechanisms of criminal justice—a trace that has not been entirely overcome, but which is enveloped, increasingly, by the non-corporal nature of the penal system" (Foucault, *Discipline and Punish: The Birth of the Prison*).

In response to Foucault and others, rehabilitation has become a popular form of addressing crime and deviance. Most North American prisons try to rehabilitate inmates through education, trades, bible studies, counseling and doing jobs within the prison. However, there are two examples within America that I believe are leaders in the field: the Prisoner Entrepreneurship Program (PEP) and the Wild Horse Program.

Established in 2004, PEP is an innovative Houston-based nonprofit organization that connects the nation's top executives, entrepreneurs, and MBA students with convicted felons. The program gives inmates the knowledge, skills and opportunities they require to succeed in the outside working world. They teach things such as academic courses, job interview skills, and even social etiquette: "[This] entrepreneurship boot camp and re-entry programs are proven solutions for preventing recidivism, maximizing self-sufficiency and transforming broken lives" (www.pep.org). The results show that "after costing the state over $20,000 per year as an inmate, the released graduates now pay an average of $7000–$10,000 per year in pay roll, sales, and income taxes and spend approximately $8 million a year in local economies" (www.pep.org). This shows that inmates improve exponentially after graduating from the PEP program and benefit greatly in many aspects of their lives. Yet although inmates gain important work and social skills, and the program has done a phenomenal job of keeping ex-prisoners out of jail—and thus maintaining a degree of social control and order—there are few details about how the individuals' overall well-being has improved.

The Wild Horse Program, on the other hand, addresses not only the human condition but the moral issue of crime. It teaches inmates "to tame wild mustangs that come right off the American plains, which will eventually be put up for adoption" (www.fusion.net). The men clean up barns and stalls, groom their horses, work with the horses in a pen, and finally, ride the newly trained horses in fields surrounding the prison fences. This "allows the inmates to form bonds with the animals, and feel the sense of accomplishment that comes from taking the task from start to finish. The effects can be lasting" (www.fusion.net). Like the PEP, it is very successful: "only about fifteen percent of the people who graduate from the program end up back in prison" (www.fusion.net). However, this program is different. It takes place in a less professional and cultured environment and has less to do with teaching prisoners how to prepare for a job interview or go about making a resume. It digs deeper, causing inmates to really question what they have been doing with their lives, for, as Dostoyevsky says: "The man who has a conscience suffers whilst acknowledging his sin. That is his punishment" (Dostoyevsky, Crime and Punishment).

The Wild Horse Program might sound like a vacation for inmates, but it improves the balance between social control and deviant behaviour. The program demonstrates what Emile Durkheim called an organic society when he developed the idea of societies becoming more complex, evolving from mechanical to organic solidarity. In organic societies, the cohesion of society depends on the individuals' dependence on each other to "perform specific tasks, although many have different values and interests" (Pfohl, Chapter Seven). Organic solidarity refers to and relies on the interdependence and components of society; each mechanism needs to work with the other in order to maintain social harmony; the more complex the society, the more integration and interdependence there is among individuals, and more cooperation and knowledge is needed. The individual, rather than the collective, is the main focus in the society, and when a crime is committed, the main focus is working on the problem and involving the individual, rather than involving the whole collective of society (Pfohl, Chapter Seven). This idea very closely relates to the Wild Horse Program because of how individually focussed they are; there is a connectedness between two different beings, the horse and its caretaker, just as there is connectedness between individuals within an organic society. In addition, the Wild Horse program focusses on individuals and helping them to grow to be stronger and better people after committing a felony.

In conclusion, both the PEP and Wild Horse programs do an excellent job of improving prisoners' well-being and maintaining social control and order. But because the Wild Horse Program creates an organic society, dealing with crime in a more individual way and working on fixing the actual problem, I believe it is more effective. Although it is necessary to have inmates learn life skills and work ethics, working on the individuals themselves—on their inner being and who they are as people—is more important. In the Wild Horse Program, inmates become connected to animals and to each other as they learn how to care for another living being. Through these connections, they become people capable of leading fulfilling lives in the complex, organic society they will return to.

## Discussion

**L**: This writer uses a number of long quotations. Are they effective and necessary?

**A**: I thought that overall, the writer used quotations as a—how do I put this? Kind of as a "get out of jail free card." He just put quotes in the middle of sentences instead of explaining the ideas in his own words and then using a quote to support that.

**L**: Can you give me an example?

**A**: Yes, there are quite a few. For example, *It teaches inmates "to tame wild mustangs that come right off the American plains, which will eventually be put up for adoption."* Then soon after that, he quotes, *This "allows the inmates to form bonds with the animals, and feel the sense of accomplishment that comes from taking the task from start to finish. The effects can be lasting."* So there are quite a few sentences that are pretty much just quotes. The quotations are just information—there's no special wording or turn of phrase that might require a quote.

As for the long quotes, I think they were somewhat overkill; the writer could have cut them down significantly and still gotten the point across. For example, the really long quote that says, *a punishment like forced labor or even imprisonment—mere loss of liberty—has never functioned without a certain additional element of punishment that certainly concerns the body itself: rationing of food, sexual deprivation, corporal punishment, solitary confinement ... There remains, therefore, a trace of "torture" in the modern mechanisms of criminal justice—a trace that has not been entirely overcome, but which is enveloped, increasingly, by the non-corporal nature of the penal system.*

I think that could probably be cut down to *a punishment like forced labor or even imprisonment—mere loss of liberty—has never functioned without a certain additional element of punishment that certainly concerns the body itself... There remains, therefore, a trace of "torture" in the modern mechanisms of criminal justice.* And I think that would have gotten the point across the same way.

**L**: Yes, I agree that most of the last sentence can be cut. But the writer's claim is that today's society is more civilized in its approach to social control, and that Foucault takes exception to these modern methods. So I feel that the details about "torturing" the body do need to be included, because the writer is saying that these elements of torture are part of our penal system. We'll have to agree to disagree on that one. Did you find another example of a quotation that is too long?

**A**: I think the first long quote in the essay could have been cut down. The problem is that I didn't completely understand it. It has a lot of big concepts that I don't have much knowledge about. But it's a paragraph in and of itself.

**L**: Yes, and when an entire paragraph is a quotation, it could be a red flag. Even though you haven't studied Foucault, you can sense that there is something wrong with the argument. What about integrating these quotations with his own language? Does this student do that?

**A**: I feel like some of the quotations weren't integrated with the writer's language. Like, some of the time, he didn't really discuss the quotes; he just put them in without discussing the concepts. The quotes in my opinion weren't used the way they should be used in an academic essay.

**L**: What did you see as the strengths of this essay?

**A**: I thought the topic was very interesting. The writer did a good job of explaining why these programs are beneficial and why he favours one over the other.

**L**: I think that's an important point, because after all, why do we write? We write for different reasons, but partly, we write for audience, and we have to think about whether the audience will find the essay interesting—and that comes back to thesis and topic selection.

Another thing I like about this essay is its structure. I like the way it flows. When you look at the previous essay, it's difficult to determine why the paragraphs are placed where they are and how they fit together. But this essay first talks about the history and theories about incarceration, and then it compares the two forms of rehabilitation. I found the essay easy to follow.

**A**: There's no bleeding paragraphs.

**L**: Yes, I thought it had a logical flow, and that's really important in academic essays.

**A**: Efficient and effective.

## Sample Essay 3

### Discovering Foucault in the Tattoo Culture

In the 1920s there were three signs of badness: socks rolled down to the ankle, long sideburns, and visible tattoos on the wrist. Tattoos were associated with gangs, sailors or street corner punks, and when media programs announced the search for wanted criminals, their tattoos were described (Dececco & Williams, 2013, p. 8). For decades in Western culture, individuals with tattoos were marred—the deviants of society, and the mainstream did not want to be associated with them: "Sociologists and other academics almost invariably described tattooing as cultural deviance. Studies of tattooing among the mentally challenged, prisoners, gang members, and deviant youth subcultures, represent the tattoo as a badge of dislocated, ostracized, and disenfranchised communities" (Atkinson, 2004, p. 126). Unmarked and undamaged bodies were the ideal: flawless, unwrinkled, skin without markings, tans, or scars reflected wealth, cleanliness and purity. Why would people pay money to have their skin permanently inked? It was a concept society couldn't understand. Michel Foucault (1990) said it well:

> If you are not like everybody else, then you are abnormal, if you are abnormal, then you are sick. These three categories, not being like everybody else, not being normal and being sick are in fact very different but have been reduced to the same thing. (p. 95)

Being physically different—and choosing to be—was a sickness. And sickness was concealed: women tattooed their lower backs or shoulder blades, and men tattooed their chests or backs—places that were easily hidden, that their mothers and bosses couldn't see, because after all, people with tattoos "were less honest, less religious, less fashionable, less athletic, less attractive and less intelligent" (Martin, 2013, p. 23). However, Foucault sees that "our current practices, supposedly grounded in sciences such as social psychology, produce anomalies such as delinquents, and then take every anomaly … as an occasion for further intervention to bring the anomalies under scientific norms. All this is done, of course, for the anomaly's own good" (Milchman, 2003, p. 43). According to Foucault, the term "normalization" standardizes anomalies and brings them under control. It doesn't only occur within government; it extends to all aspects of the individual's life and is reflected in tattoo culture.

In the latter half of the 20th century, the position of the body within popular culture began to reflect "an unprecedented individualization of the body" (Shilling, 1993, p. 1). The body became a form of self-expression, and people spent thousands of dollars on tattoos in order to display individualism and uniqueness, showcasing hobbies, stories, struggles, beliefs, journeys, and passions in a way that was formerly unheard of. "Individuals either explicitly or implicitly manage affective expression through their tattoos, thereby transforming the skin into a social billboard of normative emotion work" (Atkinson, 2004, p. 141). As Atkinson notes, it is becoming more and more popular to stage these emotions explicitly by tattooing one's body. This trend has gained force right up to the present day; it is now popular for women to get tattoos along their spines, down the sides of their ribs, around their ankles, and on their feet, wrists, and forearms. Men are likely to get full-sleeved tattoos on their legs or arms, or chest pieces, neckpieces and even tattoos along their ribs. Foucault (1991) says that

> In our society, art has become something which is related only to objects and not to individuals, or to life. That art is something which is specialized or

> which is done by experts who are artists. But couldn't everyone's life become a work of art? Why should the lamp or the house be an art object, but not our life? (p. 350)

It appears as though the tattoo culture is making our lives, or at least our bodies, works of art. Foucault (1992) defines *techniques of the self* or *arts of existence* as

> those reflective and voluntary practices by which men not only set themselves rules of conduct, but seek to transform themselves, to change themselves in their singular being, and to make their life into an oeuvre that carries certain aesthetic values and meets certain stylistic criteria. (pp. 10–11)

In current society, individuals reflect this theory of Foucault's by using tattoos as a form of self-expression and artistic illustration to "transform" themselves. Tattooing is one of the most trendy and inventive forms of individualism in the 21st century and is, as Foucault considers, a way in which art now relates to individuals, rather than just objects, as it did in the past. Yet an oeuvre must still "meet certain stylistic criteria." There are still boundaries: colours, graphics, and body placement go in and out of style. So the tattoo culture pushes against the boundaries and rules of conduct for physical appearance, always testing society's limits, wondering how far they can go before they are scrutinized. But pushing boundaries is no longer criticized; it is often respected and valued. Being different, breaking the norm, going against the grain is new and fresh. Being like everyone else is conforming, submitting to unspoken rules.

This leads to the question: how did pushing society's boundaries go from being condemned to appreciated for its innovation and originality? A "cultural and aesthetic trend now known as *postmodernism*—in art and architecture, music and film, drama and fiction—as a reflection of the present wave of political reaction is sweeping the western world" (Featherstone, 2007, p. 1). Featherstone (2007) describes postmodernism as being "strongly based on a negation of the modern, a perceived abandonment, break or shift away from the definitive features of the modern, with the emphasis firmly on the sense of the relational move away" (p. 3). Postmodernism began its incline in the late 20th century but has been fully developing within the last ten years. People began to rethink previous ideas about race, religion, ethics, society, and art. A "pathos of struggle" began, as people wanted to branch out in creative freedom. They began to "rebel against ways in which we are already defined, categorized, and classified" (Milchman, 2003, p. 69) by changing their bodies—by tattooing them—in order to see how society, people, the law, would react. They broke away from the modern era and moved into the postmodern era, where individual differences and alterations were celebrated. They began to question what was considered to be "real, necessary, or universal" (Milchman, 2003, p. 51).

But within postmodernism there are still power structures and configurations that prevent us surpassing the boundaries and keep us integrated. Foucault (2006) states that

> The real political task in a society such as ours is to criticize the workings of institutions that appear to be both neutral and independent, to criticize and attack them in such a manner that the political violence that has always exercised itself obscurely through them will be unmasked, so that one can fight against them. (p. 29)

Big and extravagant tattoos might be popular in the 21st century, but there is still a line that has been drawn to decide what is acceptable and what is considered to be taking it too far. As Foucault puts it, "we still have not cut off the head of the King" (Milchman, 2003, p. 44). When individuals have more tattooed skin than unmarked skin, people wonder what their intentions are, why they would want to look the way they do, and whether they are part of a gang or cult. But who decides what these standards are? There are no laws that decide where and how much an individual can and cannot tattoo.

Foucault (1977) says that "the judges of normality are present everywhere. We are in the society of the teacher-judge, the doctor-judge, the educator-judge, the social worker-judge" (Foucault, p. 92). These judges are the undeclared leaders and people we look up to: our managers and coworkers, our parents and family members, our professors and peers. The power they have over our choices is something Foucault (2004) calls *governmentality*:

> I would now like to start looking at that dimension which I have called by that rather nasty word "governmentality." Let us suppose that "governing" is not the same thing as "reigning," that it is not the same thing as "commanding" or "making the law," let us suppose that governing is not the same thing as being a sovereign, a suzerain, being lord, being judge, being a general, owner, master, professor. Let us suppose that there is a specificity to what it is to govern, and we must now find out a little what type of power is covered by this notion. (p. 119)

For example, in most professional careers such as corporate positions, lawyers, physicians, or pilots, tattoos are still frowned upon. If an individual is planning on becoming a family doctor, he or she knows better than to get a neck tattoo while in university. This also occurs in the service industry: flight attendants, waiters in high-class restaurants, and bank employees also cannot expose tattoos. But for other more versatile positions, such as actors, musicians, personal trainers, or baristas, tattoos are accepted and even encouraged. Many baristas at Starbucks have brightly coloured hair, facial piercings and visible tattoos because Starbucks wants to attract an artistic and trendy type of crowd. Thus, employers and managers often control the tattoo culture, impacting career choices and social standing. Family and peer influences also influence tattooing and the body. Factors such as religion, morals, ethics, and beliefs surrounding a family or peer group have a large impact on the individual. Society as a whole, then, still has standards for the tattooed population, and someone with "too many tattoos" or tattoos that are "offensive" or "unpleasant" is scrutinized and judged.

However, the tattoo culture serves to test and critique the prevailing assumptions by entering into what postmodern thinkers call a critical encounter, an *Auseinandersetzung*, a coming together and posing questions, not answering them. As Foucault says, his concern is to *open up* problems (Milchman, 2003, p.10). A critical encounter brings problems and issues into the light in order to understand them and rethink things that have always been thought to be true. However, an *Auseinandersetzung* is not a form of battle. Foucault indicates that it is the opposite of a person who is

> not a partner in the search for truth, but an adversary, an enemy who is wrong, who is harmful, and whose very existence constitutes a threat. For him, then, the game does not consist of recognizing this person as a subject having the right to speak, but of abolishing him, as interlocutor, from any possible dialogue.
> This idea that "an encounter or conflict need not lead to resolution, in which differences and not only relations are posited, in which questions are posed, not answered, in which experience is problematized, not reconciled, clashes with some of the dominant motifs in Western thought, which in its quest for Truth has privileged resolution of issues and answers to questions (Milchman, 2003, p. 11).

A critical encounter can actually build unity and be inclusive because the idea is to sharpen one another. "*Auseinandersetzung* not only tolerates the tension between division and relation, but revels in it. Its conception of strife and antagonism seeks not the calm of rational consensus, but the exhilaration of questioning and problematizing experience and thinking" (Milchman, 2003, p. 11).

Nevertheless, standards change over time, expanding and developing and pushing against boundaries. "Where there is power, there is resistance," says Foucault (1990, p. 34), and although many individuals conform to rules and limitations, feeling more secure and safe, there is always a small number of individuals who do not want to conform, especially regarding something so intimate as tattooing their bodies. Although the power governing tattoo culture isn't severe, it still exists; it is there and is always inspecting, always *surveilling*, as Foucault calls it. However, Foucault also notes that "a society without power relations can only be an abstraction" (Milchman, 2003, p. 33). Society cannot function properly without power. It cannot be operational without it. Power doesn't come only from institutions and organizations though; as Foucault says, "Power is everywhere; not because it embraces everything, but because it comes from everywhere" (Milchman, 2003, p. 44). A tattoo artist, for example, has a certain power and control over his or her clients: clients are unable to move when the artist is inking their skin and causing significant pain.

Correspondingly, the clients also have financial power over the tattoo artist, telling them what they want done, and making sure it is done properly. Both of these individuals are controlled by, and typically yield to the cultural standards, values and norms within society. For example, an individual knows better than to get a racially or religiously offensive tattoo. There is a certain influence and control here, although it is more or less unspoken.

Nonetheless, some individuals resist control and embrace scrutiny, purposely flaunting and exposing offensive tattoos and body modifications in order to invite surveillance. This gives them power: "The strategic adversary is fascism … the fascism in us all, in our heads and in our everyday behavior, the fascism that causes us to love power, to desire the very thing that dominates and exploits us" (Foucault, 1973, p. 47). Power is still everywhere, all through society, like a spirit or a presence.

Though elements of fascism exist in tattoo culture, one could also think of the tattoo artist as somewhat of an intellectual:

> The work of an intellectual is not to mold the political will of others; it is, through the analyses that he does in his own field, to re-examine evidence and assumptions, to shake up habitual ways of working and thinking, to dissipate conventional familiarities, to re-evaluate rules and institutions and to participate in the formation of a political will (where he has his role as citizen to play). (Foucault & Lotringer, 1996)

A tattoo artist is one who helps and contributes to the creation, development and construction of society through helping individuals transform their bodies into an individualistic statement. Whether the individual wants one tattoo or their entire body marked up, resisting power, the artist is the intellectual behind it, allowing the individual to make their choice. Foucault (2003) mentions that

> It is a power working to incite, reinforce, optimize, and organize the forces under it: power bent on generating forces, making them grow, and ordering them, rather than one dedicated to impeding them, making them submit, or destroying them. (p. 42)

A tattoo artist allows individuality to grow and develop within society. They create power and its ability to circulate through society. While power cannot be avoided, Foucault states that people can construct themselves within in it, something he calls "intentional creativity." Individuals can participate within power structures and enter into a critical encounter. The tattoo culture has had an enormous contribution to power and social control over the past few decades. In modern-day society, Atkinson (2004) notes

> Contemporary tattooing in Canada is, then, a social paradox and strange amalgam of cultural values about the body and its display. The tattooed body both marks long-term "civilized" cultural preferences to alter the flesh as part of "doing" social identity and signifies more recent social influences on body modification preferences arising from corporeal commodification, risk processes and technological innovation. (p. 142)

> Tattooing is the newest and most innovative form of expressing individuality, and how people choose to do so is the deciding factor about what the boundaries and limits are. Social identity is an important feature and all individuals strive for it; whether they choose to do so through tattooing is up to them. As Foucault (1994) says, "I don't write a book so that it will be the final word; I write a book so that other books are possible, not necessarily written by me" (103). A tattoo is always a book, or an opening, inviting other books to be written.

## Discussion

**L**: I found this topic to be really compelling. And topic selection is so very important. If you have a difficult theorist or you're asked to write about something that's a little over your head, a good way to deal with that is to take a modern-day phenomenon and apply it to that theorist or concept.

**A**: I agree. I didn't know anything about these concepts, so the essay did a good job of explaining them in lay terms.

**L**: What did you think of the opening line?

**A**: I really like it. It was a good hook.

**L**: That's important, isn't it? What about the introduction?

**A**: I think it does a good job of introducing society's views on tattoos: it talks about tattoos and their societal and cultural impact without saying too much about specifics that are discussed later.

**L**: What did you think of the lack of a thesis statement?

**A**: I found it confusing.

**L**: Really! I enjoyed it. I thought it was creative.

**A**: Well, now that I've read it through, it makes more sense, but as I was reading it, I didn't know what the big picture was.

**L**: Do you think that's important?

**A**: For me, yes. My brain is linear. It likes things laid out: here's what I want to say, and here's how I will say it. Because I didn't know anything about Foucault, it made it more difficult for me to see the main idea. So I think it depends on who you're writing for. It can be a very effective and interesting way to write if you're writing for an audience that knows and understands the concepts. But if you're writing for someone like me, it becomes confusing.

**L**: That's so interesting. You and I are completely different readers. I love philosophy and bunny trails, and I love wandering around with a writer. So what do you do when you have completely different readers?

**A**: I think in the end everyone writes from their own perspective, so it's easier for a linear thinker to write in a linear fashion, whereas someone who doesn't like things stated explicitly will write like that. But I think it's still about knowing your audience and writing what they need.

**L**: I guess there's a balance between being who you are as a writer and satisfying the demands of your audience. Does this writer rely too heavily on quotations, or is the essay essentially her own?

**A**: I think the writer did a good job with the quotations. If you look at the parts about tattooing, she used most of her own ideas, and she connected them with the quotes, with Foucault's ideas.

**L**: Do you have an example?

**A**: In the section that reads, *Foucault (1992) defines techniques of the self or arts of existence as those reflective and voluntary practices by which men not only set themselves rules of conduct,* *but seek to transform themselves, to change themselves in their singular being, and to make their life into an oeuvre that carries certain aesthetic values and meets certain stylistic criteria (pp. 10–11). In current society, individuals reflect this theory of Foucault's by using tattoos as a form of self-expression and artistic illustration to "transform" themselves.*

The writer takes a really difficult concept and uses her own words to explain how tattooing is an example. Another example is in the next paragraph, where the writer discusses postmodernism and its role in changing society. Then, in her own words, she ties that to tattooing.

**L**: Notice that this essay has a different organization from the previous one. That one had a block layout: first the history of rehabilitation, then two case studies: rehabilitation in prison and the Wild Horse Program. The ideas were delineated in big chunks. This essay goes deeper and deeper and deeper and pulls things in as it goes; it's like a tsunami; it keeps building. It's definitely a different style of organization. I felt that this was a nicely structured essay.

**A**: Each concept has its own paragraph, but each paragraph builds on the previous one, so the essay keeps getting deeper. You need to understand the first concept before you can understand the one that comes after it.

**L**: That's a really good point, Abigail. In the previous essay, you don't really have to know the history of incarceration in order to understand the Wild Horse Program, but in this one, you can't jump in half way. Which structure do you prefer?

**A**: The last one was more scientific, while this one is more theoretical. Honestly, I tend to write in blocks like the previous essay. But I think this structure is interesting and an effective way of dealing with difficult concepts.

**L**: It's a more sophisticated structure, creating a more powerful essay. The structure is more mature, and therefore the essay is more mature.

## Sample Essay 4

### Death and Rebirth

Laura Swart's novel *Blackbird Calling* unravels the fictional story of a young girl and her adventures with friends into the unknown. The core message is the presence of multiple characters tailoring orientation to the surroundings they are united with. *Blackbird Calling* echoes the biblical resurrection allegory, moving through life in order to meet chaos and allow it to forge rebirth.

A core biblical principle is that the old must die so that the new can come. Within this narrative, the father is the main character that resists the natural biblical allegory and clings to life, thus allowing the world to shrink into a firm collection of what he believes to be true. This is demonstrated in Father's inability to investigate chaos or the unknown which is swelling on his borders of comfort. "'Why can't they just paint, or plant a garden, for God's sake?' Father sniffed. 'That reserve is an eyesore.'" (p. 9). It appears that Father is quite concerned with others not being able to synchronize with his own views, particularly beauty. In order to reform Father's view he would have to surrender into self-denial, which is the possibility that the world is not as it seems. This exact understanding of the comfortable reality is reflected with denial of potential anarchy. "Everything is manufactured, nothing is real," Father says (p. 32). Dwelling in the known is safe and reasonable, yet it does not present the same rebirth opportunity for Father as it does to someone like Little Hummer; she is willing to face uncertainty so that she can let herself become arranged as someone who can freely march roads of the unknown.

Descent into chaos is by its nature a death, not a physical death as Christ has died but a death of the old self in hopes to exchange the old for the new. This is highlighted in the biblical message: value in the unknown, such as Israelites crossing the Red Sea. The process of dying strips down an individual and takes that person apart to a new level in which they might be built up, which is an obstacle to rebirth. Father feared the unknown for it was the centre of all uncertainty and with his own wife, he was afraid of what he might find within her: "He was afraid of what might be inside of her, I think—that part of that was hidden in tiny boxes—and it frightened him." (p. 11). Not all chaos is feared; in fact, Little Hummer demonstrates her willingness to sacrifice safety for the sake of treasures when she is willing to go in filthy places her father saw as an eyesore, both the dump and the double houses. "The pile was enormous; no limits, no horizons." Both the dump and the double houses presented themselves with very real physical danger, but to Little Hummer, danger is where her treasures are found. In many ways, Ni'is's poetry is coping and challenging the unknown; "Poetry wages war, you know. But it doesn't spill blood. Yeah I think so, it fuses horizons" (p. 78).

After finding one's treasure in dying, it is time for a rebirth or a renewal of the old self into what one hopes to become. Much like Christ, rebirth allows one to reign as a champion of danger with newfound strength and the ability to pursue greater ambitions such as future resurrection. Perhaps the greatest example of this is Ni'is's ability to understand God without putting God into a box. "You saw him outside. Outside the straight lines. I've stood in those lines, yeah. But Creator? He's like the wind. Blows where he wants to" (p. 11). Ni'is demonstrates that he can't grasp God because God pulls resurrection into an infinite cycle of knowing and necessary ignorance so that theological fundamentals can be re-evaluated. This is a parallel message to many biblical principles, both physical and non-physical resurrections: "I have been crucified with Christ and I no longer live, but Christ lives in me. The life I now live in the body, I live by faith in the Son of God" (Galatian 2:20, New International Version).

Life through death into many types of resurrection is the message of both the Gospel and *Blackbird Calling*. Little Hummer's story is not filled with these themes as universal set points but rather conflict that each character fights through in their own time; like many of the biblical heroes, some were more willing to sacrifice danger for riches. Like the phoenix the very death of Little Hummer's world allows her to fly with newfound strength she never could have experienced without taking the risk of reformation.

## Discussion

**L**: If you look at the introduction of this essay, you can see that it's too short. It's even shorter than the conclusion, which is quite rare. What can this writer add to the introduction to improve it?

**A**: I think that maybe the background of the book could have been introduced. And there are gaps between the sentences. It's a jump between the first and second sentences. Maybe the writer should have mentioned the characters and the story's central message.

**L**: What did you think about the thesis?

**A**: I thought it was too vague; words like *death*, *rebirth*, and *chaos* could mean a lot of different things. Because I've read the book, I'm able to project meaning into it. But if you're looking at it in isolation, the thesis could mean anything.

**L**: Do you think the transitions are effective?

**A**: Compared to the last few essays, there was kind of a lack. The second last paragraph connects to the one before it well, but apart from that, the paragraphs just kind of end. At least from what I can see.

**L**: I can see a somewhat logical progression: In the first paragraph the writer talks about dying, then he says that the descent into chaos is a death; then after that, he talks about treasure.

**A**: Is the first body paragraph about death or confronting the unknown? I know the writer is alluding to death, but, yes, the transitions seem—

**L**: —forced, don't you think? The previous essay really flows well, whereas in this one, the flow is artificial. In the first body paragraph, I'm a little unclear about what the author is trying to prove. Did you find that?

**A**: Yes, the topic sentence doesn't seem to be what the paragraph is about; the topic sentence says, *A core biblical principle is that the old must die so that the new can come,* but the rest of the paragraph is about *Blackbird Calling*, not about a biblical principle.

**L**: I'm also unclear about how the essay proves the thesis.

**A**: Yeah—the last sentence in the final body paragraph is the only time that the biblical side of it is ever referred to.

**L**: What about the use of quotations?

**A**: I think the use of quotations is relatively well done. The writer doesn't just put them in for the sake of putting them in; he explains their significance and not just what they mean.

**L**: Do you have an example of that?

**A**: Let's see. *"Why can't they just paint, or plant a garden, for God's sake?" Father sniffed. "That reserve is an eyesore." (p. 9). It appears that Father is quite concerned with others not being able to synchronize with his own views, particularly beauty. In order to reform Father's view he would have to surrender into self-denial, which is the possibility that the world is not as it seems. This exact understanding of the comfortable reality is reflected with denial of potential anarchy. "Everything is manufactured, nothing is real," Father says (p. 32). Dwelling in the known is safe and reasonable, yet it does not present the same rebirth opportunity for Father as it does to someone like Little Hummer.* So here, the writer explains why Father's attitude is problematic for resurrection or rebirth.

**L**: This is a really good example of **I**, don't you think? It *really* goes deep into who Father is, and I don't see that often in essays. This is an excellent example of **CSI**. Do you see how different it is from some of the other examples?

**A**: Most definitely.

**L**: What about the conclusion?

**A**: I found it interesting that in the conclusion, the writer focusses on Little Hummer even though throughout the essay, he focusses on other characters.

**L**: Do you think that's because, to this writer, Little Hummer exemplifies the rebirth narrative?

**A**: Definitely, but then why wasn't she discussed within the body of the essay to make that point?

**L**: Good point. Or perhaps we could ask why the conclusion doesn't better reflect the arguments of the essay.

## Sample Essay 5

### Examining the Syrian Refugee Crisis in Canada

In his theoretical essay "What Is a Camp," Giorgio Agamben describes what a political-juridical structure with totalitarian domination is, how it evolves, and where it has developed over the past few centuries. He begins by explaining that "camps"—which he defines as a "piece of territory that is placed outside the normal juridical order" (Agamben, 2000, p. 40)—were not born out of ordinary law or prison law, but rather from a "state of exception," a term he uses to describe a period of crisis or emergency in a nation, where the sovereign, or government, has the ability to transcend or suspend the rule of law (Agamben, 2000, p. 38). When the state of exception becomes the rule, a camp opens. In it, the state of exception, which is essentially the suspension of the state law, acquires a permanent spatial arrangement that remains outside the normal state of law (Agamben, 2000, p. 39). Agamben maintains that anything is possible within a camp because there is no law enforcement—even though the camp is created and operated by the government. He uses the concentration camps in World War Two as the most extreme example of a camp; however, he also cites events that came into being in times of crisis during the 19th and 20th centuries and claims that some gated communities in the United States are beginning to look like camps, as "political life enters a zone of absolute indeterminacy" (Agamben, 2000, p. 42). It seems improbable that Canada—a nation known to be inclusive and characterized by multiculturalism—could be a place where Agamben's notion of a camp could exist. Yet when we examine the recent Syrian refugee crisis, which brought over ten thousand refugees into Canada in the last few months of 2015, we can conclude that camps, at least to some extent are here, according to Agamben.

Within our Canadian refugee program, there are specific requirements that refugees must fulfill in order to enter the country. Refugees are detained in holding centres—operated and funded by the government—where they live until officials do a background check. If refugees seem at all suspicious, or if the Canadian Border Services Agency believes that they are at risk of escaping, or if an official is not satisfied with an individual's proof of identity, they are then sent to detainment centres (Gilbert & Loiero, 2012). According to a recent article published in CBC news, refugees claim that they feel "trapped in a prison" when they enter the country and are forced to live in these centres because of a "lack of communication, supplies, and assistance," as there is no information about when they can leave and start their lives in a new country (Hussein, 2016). Immigration Minister Jason Kenney, however, maintains that "they are not jails, and in the case of the Toronto one, it is a former three-star hotel with a fence around it. The rooms are clean, in good repair and brightly colored" (Gilbert & Loiero, 2012). Nevertheless, the facilities are surrounded by razor wire, ringing even the playground. There are bars on the windows, guards in the hallways, and surveillance cameras throughout. Mothers and children are in a separate section of the facility and can only visit with the fathers during designated visiting hours, causing difficulty and distress for the families being separated, as they initially started their journey off as families (Gilbert & Loiero, 2016). Here we see within Canada a state of exception taking place—a territory where the rights and privileges that Canadians are accustomed to are suspended.

Some of the individuals who spent time in detainment centres spoke poorly of the facilities and how they were treated, despite officials telling them that they were merely spending a few days at a "hotel." One woman who spent a week at the Toronto Immigration Holding Centre stated, "It's not just that week. It stays with you all your life. It is horrible. I don't think anyone deserves to be in a holding centre. It is jail. It was the worst week of my life" (Gilbert & Loiero, 2016). For years after being detained, many immigrants have lasting effects, with flashbacks from their short time spent in the detainment facilities; often they are frightened when they see a police officer, thinking that they are in trouble again (Gilbert & Loiero, 2016). There are also health risks for individuals living in close quarters with hundreds of others, and disease and illness spread quickly, sometimes leading to death; two men recently passed away in Ontario detainment centres due to health issues (Wyld, 2016).

All of this leads us to an important question: can immigration detainment centres be considered "camps" by Agamben's standards? Agamben (2000) stresses that a camp arises when the "political system of the modern nation state enters a period of permanent crisis and the state decides to undertake the management of the biological life of the nation directly as its own task" (p. 43). Although it is not evident that Canada has entered a period of permanent crisis, many Canadians believe that the current refugee crisis and the import of many thousands of refugees poses a risk to Canadian life and culture. In addition, it appears that government has undertaken "the management of biological life" and has stripped refugees of "every political status and reduced [them] completely to naked life" (Agamben, 2000, p. 41); refugees and immigrants are detained in crowded government-run facilities and are subject to rules about schedules, behaviour, diet, and itineraries. They have no status or rights, and as Agamben (2000) asks, "thanks to juridical procedures and political devices, how could human beings have been so completely deprived of their rights and prerogatives to the point that committing any act toward them would no longer appear as a crime?" (p. 41). It is fair to say that we do see parts of Agamben's camps in Canada's detainment centres, based on the personal accounts of individuals who have spent time in them and related them to a prison.

Furthermore, when refugees enter the country, they are immediately separated from the rest of society and forced into unknown terrain; as Agamben (2000) puts it: "the camp is a piece of territory that is placed outside the normal juridical order" (p. 40). These individuals are spatially separated because of the government's decision. As Agamben elaborates within his piece, a nation has its rules and laws, but when a camp is created and is opened up, anything can happen within. The individuals detained are essentially looked at as unequal to the rest of the country's citizens, nor are they a part of society, and in a political sense, it is not considered an offence to treat them as prisoners: "it is a measure of preventive policing inasmuch as it enabled the taking into custody of individuals regardless of any relevant criminal behavior and exclusively in order to avoid threats to the security of the state" (Agamben, 2000, p. 38). Although many refugees—especially Syrian refugees—are professionals with no record of criminal behaviour, they are suspected as a threat because they come from the war-torn Middle East. When these individuals are at risk in their native-born countries and flee to Canada, they experience the "increasingly widening gap between birth (naked life) and nation-state" (Agamben, 2000, p. 44), and that gap widens as they become spatially and socially isolated from Canadian society. Richard Ek (2006), in examining Agamben's work on camps, believes that Agamben's primary focus is on politics and the political individual: "the mythical facet departs from what Agamben regards as the primary example of inclusive exclusion in classical Western politics, namely the separation of the biological and political aspects of life" (p. 366). As the separation between the biological and political grows, so does the inequality between refugees and Canadian citizens. The political life, and rights, of refugees quickly declines when they enter Canada.

It is apparent, then, that detainment centres could be considered camps as Agamben defines them. But by looking at circumstances on a macro level, is it also possible that Canadian society in general, in the way it treats refugees who have been released from detainment centres, could also be considered a type of camp? Edward Koning and Keith Banting (2013) conducted a recent study on inequality among immigrants and refugees in Canada and concluded with the following:

> Canada has often been seen as a country that welcomes immigrants, wraps them in a multicultural blanket and supports their entry into the mainstream of Canadian life. However, stating that the immigrant's social rights are therefore guaranteed would be a hasty one. Immigrants' access to mainstream social programs is limited by direct, indirect, and informal types of exclusion. (p. 582)

The types of exclusion that Koning and Banting refer to are multiplied in the case of refugees. Laura Swart is director of refugee support for I-AM ESL, a Calgary-based educational program that supports refugees. Swart (personal communication, April 14, 2016) states that refugees coming into Canada are provided with funding, education, basic living needs, and social assistance. On the surface, she says, it appears that we as a nation are supporting these individuals and helping them to integrate into mainstream society. Yet this is far from the reality; refugees are often placed on waiting lists for English classes, are given a single blanket to warm them in the winter months, cannot afford to buy fresh produce or ethnic food, and often suffer from post-traumatic stress, for which they are not being treated. Furthermore, if they are disabled or caring for a person with a disability, they are essentially housebound. Women are particularly vulnerable; with long waiting lists for childcare, they cannot attend school to learn the language and often remain in their homes, venturing only to the nearby Superstore or playground. In addition, they are often subject to domestic abuse and have no family support (Swart, personal communication, April 14, 2016). Consequently, even though most refugees eventually move into their own homes, they still experience spatial, social, and emotional isolation and cannot access the resources that other Canadians enjoy. They congregate in specific areas, speak their own language, practice their own customs, and sometimes follow their own laws—some of which conflict with Canadian laws (Swart, personal communication, April 14, 2016).

Given the current situation with Syrian refugees, it is reasonable to say that Canada can be seen in some ways as a camp, if we are following Agamben's theories. Agamben says that a camp is a space that opens up when the state of exception starts to become the rule and the State decides to undertake the management of the biological life as its own task. Canada has done exactly this by opening up the country to refugees when they are in a state of exception and managing them as individuals. Furthermore, when totalitarian domination occurs within a camp, any sort of treatment is permitted. Even though Agamben applies this example to more extreme situations such as prisoner of war camps and concentration camps, in Canada, the main features of his theory are certainly evident in the strategies we use to assist refugees. Regardless of whether these individuals are placed in a detainment centre or granted citizenship, they face exclusion and separation from the rest of society and lack basic privileges that Canadian-born citizens are granted. In some cases they are subject to inappropriate treatment, which the government feels is necessary for the sake of national security. Canada may not have some of the extremities that Agamben elaborates on in his piece; however, with some of the basic characteristics matching up to Agamben's theory, it causes us to wonder what it is like living in the country from a refugee's perspective.

## Discussion

**A**: This essay I found easier to read than the other ones because I understand the concepts; I've read Agamben.

**L**: Yes, of course!

**A**: I thought the writer did a very good job of describing Agamben's theories. Even before I had delved into Agamben, I read this essay and I still understood it. The writer uses a lot of references to the text and explains them, which is very good.

**L**: Can you give me an example of how she does that?

**A**: The second sentence: *[Agamben] begins by explaining that "camps"—which he defines as a "piece of territory that is placed outside the normal juridical order...."* The writer then explains this quotation, or expands on it in the next few sentences.

**L**: But the next few sentences are a paraphrase, not the writer's own thinking.

**A**: True, but at the same time, to paraphrase Agamben's ideas—I found Agamben's theories really difficult; I had to reference outside sources in order to understand them. So even though it's a paraphrase, the ability to take Agamben's ideas and make them understandable to someone who doesn't know them? Well done!

**L**: Good point, Abigail. Is there another example of **CSI** that is used well? I think we've established that this writer makes effective claims and supports them, but is there an example in which she voices her own ideas?

**A**: Probably when she introduces the refugee crisis; her claim is that camps are present with refugees, and for the rest of the essay, she backs that up.

**L**: So this writer uses an example from the present day to delineate Agamben's theories. And that prevents her from plagiarizing or just paraphrasing, because an essay is more than paraphrasing. So it's helpful to apply a difficult theory to a modern-day phenomenon.

**A**: Yes, it helps you to use the **I** in **CSI**. What does **I** stand for again?

**L**: Any **I** will do: interpretation, investigation, imagination.

[*Laughter.*]

As an instructor, I'm often concerned about the lack of critical thinking in student writing. Many students don't think for themselves—especially when delineating the theories of someone like Agamben; their essays are just one quotation after another. But if students can learn how to say something about the quotations, they will be less likely to plagiarize. And I think that applying a theory to a new situation is one way of doing that. For example, in your research essay, you're applying Agamben's theories about camps to people who suffer from dementia.

**A**: Yes, and it fits so well. I thought it would be much more difficult.

**L**: Do you think this writer effectively balances Agamben's theories with data from the refugee crisis?

**A**: I think it is balanced quite well; there's a mix between quotations from Agamben and her own research and ideas; they go back and forth.

**L**: And of course, you have an example to support that.

**A**: One example would be that she describes detainment centres as *camps*—as Agamben defines them.

**L**: Does this essay prove its thesis, that Canada has essentially created *camps* in dealing with the refugee crisis?

**A**: I think it does a good job of proving the thesis. It directly connects Agamben's ideas with the refugee situation. But I also think the essay only addresses a few of Agamben's theories about what a camp is; it really only focuses on the political separation. It proves that the refugee crisis creates camps to some degree, but possibly not all the way, if that makes sense.

**L**: Yes, I think you bring up another good point, and again, this is a flaw that I see in some essays—the writer only touches on part of the theory that she is asked to write about. This essay states that the refugee crisis is creating Agamben-like camps; therefore, as you say, the writer should be talking about all of the significant terms relevant to camps; not just a select few. If students are asked to discuss five terms, many will talk about two or three at length and either forget the others or give them lip service. It kind of goes back to the importance of answering the question posed.

## Sample Essay 6

### Policing the Body

For many years, there has been pressure placed upon athletes—especially female athletes—to maintain a specific body weight and size in order to perform to the maximum of their abilities within their sport. Whether it is their coaches, their teammates, their parents, or society, many females feel pressured to discipline their bodies to maintain the perfect shape. They become, as Erving Goffman's theory of dramaturgy describes it, actors on the stage of life, spending most of their time on the front stage performing to the best of their ability in an attempt to impress those watching. Their performance and how they appear while performing is crucial, and they will do whatever it takes in order to maintain the impression of a strong, healthy athlete.

In the article "Slimming Down for Sport: Developing a Weight Pressures in Sport Measure for Female Athletes," Justine J. Reel, Sonya SooHoo, Trent A. Petrie, Christy Greenleaf, and Jennifer E. Carter develop the idea that "the focus on appearance inside and outside of the sport can lead athletes to feel pressured to fit a body ideal for sport and society" (Reel et al. 2010, p. 100). Disciplining the body is one of the most important aspects of being an athlete, and whether that means gaining muscle or shedding weight, athletes feel the pressure from inside and outside sources to reach their peak performance levels. Their bodies are diligently watched and monitored by judges, coaches, teammates, fans, and peers; they are examined and policed from head to toe.

Yet according to the American College of Sport Medicine (ACSM), in Michael Brunet's article "Female Athlete Triad," close monitoring of the body appears to be more common in certain types of sports. In sports where performance is subjectively scored, such as dance, figuring skating, and gymnastics, female bodies reflect society's concept of a thin, graceful swan in order to look elegant and appealing in the eyes of the audience. Endurance sports such as distance running, cycling, and cross-country skiing favour participants who have low body weight, and athletes who wear body contour-revealing clothing for competition (in sports such as volleyball, swimming, and diving) are closely monitored, even though their counterparts in hockey or basketball are rarely pressured to be thin. No one will notice an extra ten pounds under a padded hockey uniform or a baggy basketball uniform.

Most female athletes will go to great lengths in order to maintain the body-type that is expected in their sport, even if it means putting their health at risk. For example, the female athlete triad is a serious disorder that affects as many as 62 percent of female athletes. It begins with an eating disorder, usually either bulimia or anorexia, and in time, athletes begin to have irregular, prolonged and even discontinued menstrual cycles because they are lacking nutrients, calories, and aren't maintaining a healthy body weight. The absence of menstrual cycles then leads to osteoporosis and loss of bone density/mass because the body is lacking its daily intake of vitamins, as well as estrogen and progesterone (Brunet, 623–632).

As an athlete on the school's varsity swim team, I have personal experience with this issue. Our coach has addressed the issue of weight with more than half of the females on the team (but hardly any of the males), suggesting that if we lost 10–15 pounds and were more conscious of what we ate, we would perform better. None of us has succumbed to an eating disorder or the female athlete triad, but we are all cautious about what we eat, how much we eat, and we weigh ourselves regularly. We feel pressured to meet our coach's standards, the university's standards, and the standards of our peers, who view us as athletes; we want to represent the athletics of our school in a way that makes people proud. Although our coach isn't forceful or persistent in the matter and doesn't threaten to cut us from the team if we are too heavy by his standards, many other coaches and athletics are like this, and the demand for "the perfect figure" is much more intense.

This leads to an important question: how and why do others control what female athletes do with their bodies? Erving Goffman's theories about impression management show that on stage, people manage their clothing, words, and nonverbal actions to give a particular impression to others. Goffman describes each individual's "performance" as the presentation of self, a person's efforts to create specific impressions in the minds of others (Brayton, January 15). Female athletes are no exception. When teammates, coaches, even society—the audience—pressure them to look a certain way in order to perform a certain way, athletes make adjustments in the backstage portion of their lives, and for some, this develops into serious eating disorders. When they come back onto the front stage, looking the way the audience wants them to, they may not perform to their potential because they have manipulated the audience into thinking that they have developed the perfect athlete's body in a healthy and beneficial way. Yet Goffman also says that humans *choose* to manipulate and influence the way others see them when they are on front stage. The athlete partners with the audience and agrees to play an idealized role in order to succeed, in order to be included, admired, and accepted.

In conclusion, female athletes can be seen as actors on stage, performing for those watching and policing their bodies. If they do not meet the audience's expectations, they change themselves; they create the impression of a healthy, athletic body. But in the end, the way in which female athletes govern and discipline their bodies is their own choice: they have the power to decide for themselves, despite society's influence and pressure, how much they will modify their bodies in order to be part of the athletic community.

## Discussion

**L**: This essay opens with a description of how athletes' bodies are being policed—especially athletes such as ballerinas or swimmers. The essay then narrows to a discussion about how policing affects females, then it describes a personal experience, and finally, it poses questions about who makes the decisions regarding what an athlete should look like. What do you think of the overall structure, and specifically, of where the writer has slotted the personal anecdote?

**A**: I wasn't sure if it belongs in the paper. It's dependent on what type of paper it is, because I think the anecdote is good; it provides real-world examples of abstract concepts. It provides relatability; you can see it happening rather than just being told it happens. I think it provides some knowledge on the negative effects of policing the body.

**L**: Let's assume that the professor encouraged students to use personal anecdotes. Did you think that the anecdote is jarring after the theory, or do you like where it is placed? Should it have been placed at the beginning?

**A**: No, I don't think it should be at the beginning, because you need the theory first. I did find it a little sudden, but that's because I'm not accustomed to seeing personal anecdotes in essays—I personally try to avoid them. But I think it provides good context.

**L**: Yes, I think sometimes we have the idea in academia that well-known theorists are the only valid sources of information; their opinions, their words are highly valued, and what can an undergraduate student possibly add to the discussion? But in this essay, we see that a first-year student has a great deal of understanding about the topic—as much as a published writer has.

How effectively does the writer develop Erving Goffman's theories about impression management?

**A**: I think that the ideas could have been developed more. I think it would have been more effective if they were referenced throughout the piece rather than simply in the final paragraph.

**L**: Oh! That's interesting!

**A**: The last paragraph is the only one that delves into his ideas; they're introduced in the introduction but aren't mentioned again until the last paragraph. So I almost found that transition to be harder than the transition into the personal anecdote, because Goffman's theories are big concepts that hadn't been explained, and I was trying to connect them to the previous parts of the essay that had been explained.

**L**: Okay, but how would you do that?

**A**: Well, the writer uses some interesting metaphors in this last paragraph, and expanding on those throughout the rest of the body of the essay could have been beneficial. It doesn't seem like it would be too difficult to integrate. For example, *Goffman describes each individual's "performance" as the presentation of self, a person's efforts to create specific impressions in the minds of others* could probably fit after the topic sentence of the second body paragraph: *Yet according to the American College of Sport Medicine (ACSM), in Michael Brunet's article "Female Athlete Triad," close monitoring of the body appears to be more common in certain types of sports.* Then she could talk about how people put on different types of performances in different sports, using Goffman's ideas throughout.

**L**: That gives me something to think about. This particular writer is a linear thinker—she likes order—and I think this impacts how she constructs her essays. I wonder if she would find it difficult to follow your suggestion simply because her brain doesn't work that way.

**A**: Possibly. But I think if the assignment asks you to connect ideas, then the majority of the essay needs to be about connecting those ideas rather than discussing one idea, then the next idea.

**L**: Good point. I think that after this discussion, we'll both be better essayists, Abigail!

**A**: I agree. I think it's very beneficial.

# 16

# Conclusion

Allow me to end with an anecdote. A few years ago, I was given the rich opportunity of teaching Indigenous students at the University of Calgary. My students and I teamed up with Professor Lonnie Graham of Pennsylvania State University to create a photo exhibit that depicted what it means to be Indigenous in Canada. University faculty and students came to the exhibit. Members of the community came. They asked questions. And suddenly, my students became the primary sources that other students used for their research papers; my students became the authorities. Their words were valued, and it was transformative for us all.

You also have something to say.

Writing is hard work, yes—but it's not *beyond* you, because it comes *from* you. Don't flutter around robust theorists; *enter into them* and say things—things that create openings, things that will transform your readers, if you will take the leap. As Søren Kierkegaard says, "To dare is to lose one's footing momentarily. Not to dare is to lose oneself."

# APPENDIX 1
# Bedouin

ROBERT LACEY

It is sunrise in the desert. The sky is grey, the wind is cold. The camels cough and gurgle, irked by the thongs that hobble their forelegs. And on the carpet in front of one of the black goat-hair tents is a boy making coffee.

As he puts wood on the fire he calls for water and for coffee beans, and over the embroidered hanging that shuts off the women's section of the tent a hand passes them to him silently. He puts the water in a blackened brass coffee pot to boil. The beans, dry and greenish, he roasts in a shallow open pan.

Their aroma has barely started to rise when he tosses them, pale brown, into a heavy brass mortar, and, as they cool, he pounds them hard, striking the side of the mortar with alternate blows to make a bell-like sound. The ringing echoes round the camp, and robed men start sauntering to the fire. They sit cross-legged, feet bare. The elders lean on the sheepskin of a camel saddle, watching the sun slowly warm and color the landscape.

Now the boy is calling for cardamom seeds, and another hand—or is it the same one?—passes the grey pods to him over the divider. He pounds the spice hard into the mortar, tipping its fibrous dust into the pot, and, when coffee and cardamom have boiled together three times, he puts a twist of date palm coir into the spout. This strains the liquid and he samples it, dashing a few drops into a small handleless cup.

He takes up a stack of these little cups, balancing them one inside the other on his right hand, while he grasps the pot in his left, and then he walks around the circle, pouring out thimblefuls of the cloudy green-brown liquor.

When the men want more they hold out their cup. When they have had enough, they hold out their cup again, but this time they waggle it from side to side. Then the boy takes the cup back into the bottom of his stack and stays standing until the last man has finished.

It could be dawn any morning in the deserts of modern Sa'udi Arabia—pick-up trucks parked beside the black goat-hair tents, a plastic and chrome cassette radio wailing out music on the rich woven carpet. But it is nearly a century ago, somewhere in eastern Arabia, and the boy making coffee is Abdul Aziz ibn Sa'ud, the founder of the Kingdom.

The Al Sa'ud are refugees. Rulers of Riyadh for decades, they have been evicted from their town by the rival dynasty of Rasheed, and now they possess no more than they can strap on the backs of their camels, itinerates like the wandering tribesman or dung beetle, pushing their worldly wealth across the blistered face of the wilderness. It is the spring of 1891.

# APPENDIX 2
# Marrakech

GEORGE ORWELL

As the corpse went past the flies left the restaurant table in a cloud and rushed after it, but they came back a few minutes later.

The little crowd of mourners—all men and boys, no women—threaded their way across the market-place between the piles of pomegranates and the taxis and the camels, wailing a short chant over and over again. What really appeals to the flies is that the corpses here are never put into coffins, they are merely wrapped in a piece of rag and carried on a rough wooden bier on the shoulders of four friends. When the friends get to the burying-ground they hack an oblong hole a foot or two deep, dump the body in it and fling over it a little of the dried-up, lumpy earth, which is like broken brick. No gravestone, no name, no identifying mark of any kind. The burying-ground is merely a huge waste of hummocky earth, like a derelict building-lot. After a month or two no one can even be certain where his own relatives are buried.

When you walk through a town like this—two hundred thousand inhabitants, of whom at least twenty thousand own literally nothing except the rags they stand up in—when you see how the people live, and still more how easily they die, it is always difficult to believe that you are walking among human beings. All colonial empires are in reality founded upon that fact. The people have brown faces—besides, there are so many of them! Are they really the same flesh as yourself? Do they even have names? Or are they merely a kind of undifferentiated brown stuff, about as individual as bees or coral insects? They rise out of the earth, they sweat and starve for a few years, and then they sink back into the nameless mounds of the graveyard and nobody notices that they are gone. And even the graves themselves soon fade back into the soil. Sometimes, out for a walk, as you break your way through the prickly pear, you notice that it is rather bumpy underfoot, and only a certain regularity in the bumps tells you that you are walking over skeletons.

I was feeding one of the gazelles in the public gardens.

Gazelles are almost the only animals that look good to eat when they are still alive, in fact, one can hardly look at their hindquarters without thinking of mint sauce. The gazelle I was feeding seemed to know that this thought was in my mind, for though it took the piece of bread I was holding out it obviously did not like me. It nibbled rapidly at the bread, then lowered its head and tried to butt me, then took another nibble and then butted again. Probably its idea was that if it could drive me away the bread would somehow remain hanging in mid-air.

An Arab navvy working on the path nearby lowered his heavy hoe and sidled towards us. He looked from the gazelle to the bread and from the bread to the gazelle, with a sort of quiet amazement, as though he had never seen anything quite like this before. Finally he said shyly in French:

"*I* could eat some of that bread."

I tore off a piece and he stowed it gratefully in some secret place under his rags. This man is an employee of the Municipality.

When you go through the Jewish quarters you gather some idea of what the medieval ghettoes were probably like. Under their Moorish rulers the Jews were only allowed to own land in certain restricted areas, and after centuries of this kind of treatment they have ceased to bother about overcrowding. Many of the streets are a good deal less than six feet wide, the houses are completely windowless, and sore-eyed children cluster everywhere in unbelievable numbers, like clouds of flies. Down the centre of the street there is generally running a little river of urine.

In the bazaar huge families of Jews, all dressed in the long black robe and little black skull-cap, are working in dark fly-infested booths that look like caves. A carpenter sits cross-legged at a prehistoric lathe, turning chair-legs at lightning speed. He works the lathe with a bow in his right hand and guides the chisel with his left foot, and thanks to a lifetime of sitting in this position his left leg is warped out of shape. At his side his grandson, aged six, is already starting on the simpler parts of the job.

I was just passing the coppersmiths' booths when somebody noticed that I was lighting a cigarette. Instantly, from the dark holes all round, there was a frenzied rush of Jews, many of them old grandfathers with flowing grey beards, all clamouring for a cigarette. Even a blind man somewhere at the back of one of the booths heard a rumour of cigarettes and came crawling out, groping in the air with his hand. In about a minute I had used up the whole packet. None of these people, I suppose, works less than twelve hours a day, and every one of them looks on a cigarette as a more or less impossible luxury.

As the Jews live in self-contained communities they follow the same trades as the Arabs, except for agriculture. Fruit-sellers, potters, silversmiths, blacksmiths, butchers, leather-workers, tailors, water-carriers, beggars, porters—whichever way you look you see nothing but Jews. As a matter of fact there are thirteen thousand of them, all living in the space of a few acres. A good job Hitler isn't here. Perhaps he is on his way, however. You hear the usual dark rumours about the Jews, not only from the Arabs but from the poorer Europeans.

"Yes, *mon vieux*, they took my job away from me and gave it to a Jew. The Jews! They're the real rulers of this country, you know. They've got all the money. They control the banks, finance—everything."

"But," I said, "isn't it a fact that the average Jew is a labourer working for about a penny an hour?"

"Ah, that's only for show! They're all money-lenders really. They're cunning, the Jews."

In just the same way, a couple of hundred years ago, poor old women used to be burned for witchcraft when they could not even work enough magic to get themselves a square meal.

All people who work with their hands are partly invisible, and the more important the work they do, the less visible they are. Still, a white skin is always fairly conspicuous. In northern Europe, when you see a labourer ploughing a field, you probably give him a second glance. In a hot country, anywhere south of Gibraltar or east of Suez, the chances are that you don't even see him. I have noticed this again and again. In a tropical landscape one's eye takes in everything except the human beings. It takes in the dried-up soil, the prickly pear, the palm-tree and the distant mountain, but it always misses the peasant hoeing at his patch. He is the same colour as the earth, and a great deal less interesting to look at.

It is only because of this that the starved countries of Asia and Africa are accepted as tourist resorts. No one would think of running cheap trips to the Distressed Areas. But where the human beings have brown skins their poverty is simply not noticed. What does Morocco mean to a Frenchman? An orange-grove or a job in government service. Or to an Englishman? Camels, castles, palm-trees, Foreign Legionnaires, brass trays and bandits. One could probably live here for years without noticing that for nine-tenths of the people the reality of life is an endless, back-breaking struggle to wring a little food out of an eroded soil.

Most of Morocco is so desolate that no wild animal bigger than a hare can live on it. Huge areas which were once covered with forest have turned into a treeless waste where the soil is exactly like broken-up brick. Nevertheless a good deal of it is cultivated, with frightful labour. Everything is done by hand. Long lines of women, bent double like inverted capital Ls, work their way slowly across the fields, tearing up the prickly weeds with their hands, and the peasant gathering lucerne for fodder pulls it up stalk by stalk instead of reaping it, thus saving an inch or two on each stalk. The plough is a wretched wooden thing, so frail that one can easily carry it on one's shoulder, and fitted underneath with a rough iron spike which stirs the soil to a depth of about four inches. This is as much as the strength of the animals is equal to. It is usual to plough with a cow and a donkey yoked together. Two donkeys would not be quite strong enough, but on the other hand two cows would cost a little more to feed. The peasants possess no harrows, they merely plough the soil several times over in different directions, finally leaving it in rough furrows, after which the whole field has to be shaped with hoes into small oblong patches, to conserve water. Except for a day or two after the rare rainstorms there is never enough water. Along the edges of the fields channels are hacked out to a depth of thirty or forty feet to get at the tiny trickles which run through the subsoil.

Every afternoon a file of very old women passes down the road outside my house, each carrying a load of firewood. All of them are mummified with age and the sun, and all of them are tiny. It seems to be generally the case in primitive communities that the women, when they get beyond a certain age, shrink to the size of children. One day a poor old creature who could not have been more than four feet tall crept past me under a vast load of wood. I stopped her and put a five-sou piece (a little more than a farthing) into her hand. She answered with a shrill wail, almost a scream, which was partly gratitude but mainly surprise. I suppose that from her point of view, by taking any notice of her, I seemed almost to be violating a law of nature. She accepted her status as an old woman, that is to say as a beast of burden. When a family is travelling it is quite usual to see a father and a grown-up son riding ahead on donkeys, and an old woman following on foot, carrying the baggage.

But what is strange about these people is their invisibility. For several weeks, always at about the same time of day, the file of old women had hobbled past the house with their firewood, and though they had registered themselves on my eyeballs I cannot truly say that I had seen them. Firewood was passing—that was how I saw it. It was only that one day I happened to be walking behind them, and the curious up-and-down motion of a load of wood drew my attention to the human being underneath it. Then for the first time I noticed the poor old earth-coloured bodies, bodies reduced to bones and leathery skin, bent double under the crushing weight. Yet I suppose I had not been five minutes on Moroccan soil before I noticed the overloading of the donkeys and was infuriated by it. There is no question that the donkeys are damnably treated. The Moroccan donkey is hardly bigger than a St. Bernard dog, it carries a load which in the British army would be considered too much for a fifteen-hands mule, and very often its pack-saddle is not taken off its back for weeks together. But what is peculiarly pitiful is that it is the most willing creature on earth, it follows its master like a dog and does not need either bridle or halter. After a dozen years of devoted work it suddenly drops dead, whereupon its master tips it into the ditch and the village dogs have torn its guts out before it is cold.

This kind of thing makes one's blood boil, whereas—on the whole—the plight of the human beings does not. I am not commenting, merely pointing to a fact. People with brown skins are next door to invisible. Anyone can be sorry for the donkey with its galled back, but it is generally owing to some kind of accident if one even notices the old woman under her load of sticks.

As the storks flew northward the Negroes were marching southward—a long, dusty column, infantry, screw-gun batteries and then more infantry, four or five thousand men in all, winding up the road with a clumping of boots and a clatter of iron wheels.

They were Senegalese, the blackest Negroes in Africa, so black that sometimes it is difficult to see whereabouts on their necks the hair begins. Their splendid bodies were hidden in reach-me-down khaki uniforms, their feet squashed into boots that looked like blocks of wood, and every tin hat seemed to be a couple of sizes too small. It was very hot and the men had marched a long way. They slumped under the weight of their packs and the curiously sensitive black faces were glistening with sweat.

As they went past a tall, very young Negro turned and caught my eye. But the look he gave me was not in the least the kind of look you might expect. Not hostile, not contemptuous, not sullen, not even inquisitive. It was the shy, wide-eyed Negro look, which actually is a look of profound respect. I saw how it was. This wretched boy, who is a French citizen and has therefore been dragged from the forest to scrub floors and catch syphilis in garrison towns, actually has feelings of reverence before a white skin. He has been taught that the white race are his masters, and he still believes it.

But there is one thought which every white man (and in this connection it doesn't matter twopence if he calls himself a Socialist) thinks when he sees a black army marching past. "How much longer can we go on kidding these people? How long before they turn their guns in the other direction?"

It was curious, really. Every white man there has this thought stowed somewhere or other in his mind. I had it, so had the other onlookers, so had the officers on their sweating chargers and the white NCOs marching in the ranks. It was a kind of secret which we all knew and were too clever to tell; only the Negroes didn't know it. And really it was almost like watching a flock of cattle to see the long column, a mile or two miles of armed men, flowing peacefully up the road, while the great white birds drifted over them in the opposite direction, glittering like scraps of paper.

*1939*

# References

Agamben, Giorgio (2000). *Means without end: Notes on politics*. (Vincenzo Binetti and Cesare Casarino, Trans.). Minneapolis & London: Minnesota Press.

Chomsky, Noam (1971). *Human nature: Justice versus power*. Retrieved from https://chomsky.info/1971xxxx/

Foucault, Michel (1972). *The archaeology of knowledge*. New York: Random House.

Foucault, Michel (1977). *Language, counter-memory, practice: Selected essays and interviews*. New York: Cornell University Press.

Gadamer, Hans-Georg (1997). *Truth and method*. (Joel Weinsheimer and Donald G. Marshall, Trans). New York: Continuum.

Lacey, Robert (1981). *The kingdom*. New York: Harcourt Brace Jovanovich.

McCann, Colum (2017). *Letters to a young writer*. New York: Random House.

Orwell, George (2003). *Marrakech*. Retrieved from http://www.george-orwell.org/Marrakech/0.html

Swart, Laura (2016). *Blackbird Calling*. Toronto: Quattro.

Swart, Laura (2019). *Ransomed*. Toronto: Guernica Editions.

# About the Author

Author Laura Swart is passionate about writing and teaching. She has taught academic writing to post-secondary students for over twenty years, encouraging them to find and raise their writing voices. She is a published novelist and playwright and the director of I-AM ESL, an online language school that uses story and song to teach the intri cacies of English to refugees. Laura's degrees and research in education, philosophy, and theology have shaped her pedagogy, and the theories of Hans-Georg Gadamer in particular have woven themselves into her thinking, her teaching, and her writing. Find out more about Laura's books at www.swartbooks.com.

# About the Illustrator

Barbara Lamb has a diploma in art and design from Red Deer College. After a widely varied career, she started her own company, Imaginations Ink, working as both a graphic designer and a visual artist. Her art concentrates on portraiture and still life. Travel has been a significant influence on Barbara's work, which can be found in private collections in Canada, the United States, Scotland, and Australia. She currently lives and paints in Calgary, Alberta. You can learn more about Barbara at www.BarbaraLambArt.com.